A Journey from T1 Relationships to Personal Freedom

Dr. Winston Collins

ISBN: 1497326354
ISBN 13: 9781497326354
Library of Congress Control Number: 2014905105
CreateSpace Independent Publishing Platform
North Charleston, South Carolina

Next Dimension Recovery Press

SPECIAL DEDICATION

I thank Dr. Robert Bass, Jr., Physician and Attorney, for taking me under your powerful wings and teaching me how to fly. I thank you for everything you taught me and most importantly, how to **think.** *I will always love you and your spirit will always be a part of me. I miss you. I dedicate this book to you Dr. Bass.*

I thank Harvie and Veada Collins, my parents. I dedicate this book to you and I appreciate the sacrifices you made for me and my siblings. This book is a product of your hard work and unconditional love. Thank you mom and dad.

ACKNOWLEDGEMENTS

I would like to thank my many clients who, over the past 25 years, taught me and helped me to grow as a professional. As a new University of Pennsylvania graduate, you helped me understand your lived experiences through your lenses. I have gleaned vicarious knowledge from your struggles in life. I am now able to tell your story from a healthy perspective. The lessons you taught me were invaluable at building my clinical knowledge and skills. You inspired me to write this book. You know who you are and I thank you all.

TABLE OF CONTENTS

PREFACE

The need for this book became apparent to me during my work with individuals and families in my private counseling practice. My practice began shortly after I received my doctorate from the University of Pennsylvania in 1984. I saw an average of 20 clients per week during evening hours. They were people from all walks of life including postal workers, attorneys, physicians, nurses, bus drivers, police officers, children and retired persons. They were diverse in terms of age, race, culture, gender and sexual orientation. They presented an array of mental health and substance abuse challenges. Their primary concern was problems with their family relationships.

I spent the first five years largely listening to them and providing clinical feedback. After five years, I began to notice they were not responding to traditional 'therapies' as well as I expected. It was then that I realized much of what was being reported by these individuals and families simply did not make sense. Initially, I believed it made sense because they were telling me about their own life experiences. I believed they were the experts of their own life experiences. However, when I began to challenge their view of themselves and their relationships, I discovered that very little of their stories added up. They were seeing things that were not evident to me.

I had recently completed a dissertation based on self concept. I knew a lot about self theory, self formation and how the perceptions of others are internalized to define the self. I understood that people's misperceptions of themselves would adversely impact their relationship with themselves and others. I began to suspect that my clients had low self concept. They had poor interaction with self. How could they interact well with others? I was skilled at the use of the Tennessee Self Concept Scale (TSCS) by Fitts and Warren. I administered and scored over 600 TSCSs while collecting data for my dissertation. In 1990, I began to use it as a clinical tool to measure the self concept of my clients. I found that a majority of my clients had a T score of 44 or below, which is indicative of low self-concept. Since one's self concept does not fluctuate, I knew the injury to the self concept of my adult clients occurred many years earlier.

By 2005, I learned a wealth of information from the experiences of my clients. I developed clinical interventions that helped them restore a healthy self concept. I used the TSCS as a post-test to support clinical findings of improvement in self concept (T score of 45 or above). Improvement in self concept helped my clients to recover from addictive behaviors; trauma; mental health challenges; and their problems with relationships.

I was not aware of other professionals focusing on the specific type of work I was doing. I felt individuals and families were under-served by existing programs and resources. I decided to fill this informational void to help reduce human suffering.

In 2005, I started a monthly group forum called Next Dimension Recovery (NDR). The purpose of this forum was to help people build self esteem and develop healthy relationships. We met at a local church in the Germantown section of Philadelphia, Pa. By word of mouth, people began to attend the forums where I spoke on subjects related to self and relationships. NDR was an effective way to get this information across to large numbers of people, some in recovery and others not involved in recovery. Many people reported the psycho-educational information presented at the forums was extremely helpful to them.

After seven years (2012) of hard and dedicated effort, I completed my purpose for NDR and continued to utilize the information in my private practice, which I still operate. Fortunately, all of my forums were captured on DVD or CD. In 2013, I decided to reduce this life changing material to writing and share it with people all over America, and possibly the world. I introduce to you **'A Journey from T1 Relationships to Personal Freedom'**. I have found this to be an amazing and rewarding experience. I am grateful for this greater opportunity to help individuals and families improve their lives and relationships.

INTRODUCTION

One of the most prevalent social phenomena in America today is troubled relationships. Parents are at odds with each other; children are at odds with their parents; children are bullying other children; families are in chaos; couples spend more time arguing than communicating with each other; young people are turning to a relationship with drugs at alarming rates; and there is no end in sight. Some have capitalized on the 'pandemic' of troubled relationships with reality shows; sit-coms; talk shows; court television shows; and movies. Troubled relationships appear to be the norm in society because 'everyone' seems to have a troubled relationship. The family is at the core of any society. When the family is sick, society cannot be well.

This book is written to cast light upon **T1 relationships**. While troubled relationships may look similar on the surface, T1 relationships are unique and wreak havoc upon the lives of individuals and families across America. T1 relationships are a root cause of family dissolution and erosion of the social fabric of our communities. While no one talks about T1 relationships, adults and children are hurting. Discussion of T1 relationships has been the proverbial 4000 pound elephant in the room that no one sees or talks about. There is ample discussion on gun control laws; holding schools and teachers more accountable; and/or increased funding for more prisons. T1 relationships are omitted from conferences, workshops and other discussions on the family; domestic violence; poor academic performance of our children; crime; and the drug epidemic. A discussion of T1 relationships is virtually overlooked, until now. T1 relationships make significant contributions to:

» poor communication in the family;

» the inability to establish intimate relationships;

» difficulty establishing trust;

» loneliness;

» the growing trend toward work-a-holism to avoid emotional responsibility;

» silent guilt and shame;

» generalized fear and anxiety;

» inability to 'fit-in';

» feelings of anger/resentment; and

» the inability to answer the basic question, '**Who am I**?'

The T1 relationship phenomenon is a factor contributing to depression, overeating, gambling, substance abuse challenges, and other public health and social problems. This book will help potentially millions of children and adults to no longer suffer in silence in all corners of our society. A rigorous discussion of T1 relationships begins **here**. You can be a part of this discussion if you are in a T1 relationship; if you are a behavioral health professional; or if you have a general interest in why people behave the way they do.

For those who may be involved in a T1 relationship, let's take a brief look at your 'knowledge' and make sure it does not interfere with your ability to receive the information you will need for your Journey from T1 Relationships to Personal Freedom.

WHAT YOU KNOW

Knowledge is great; but sometimes, knowledge can be self defeating. Some people say, 'I know this and I know that'; or 'I already know this, and 'I already know that'. If you add up all that you know and then take a look at what your knowledge has produced, you may see that your life has become stuck and disappointing. It is critically important that you not allow what you already know to become a low ceiling. You can become imprisoned by what you know. At this time, do not focus on what you **know**; focus on what you **don't know**.

Several years ago, I met a guy whose life dream was to become a master plumber. Prior to becoming a master plumber, he was a novice at plumbing. He could not achieve his life dream simply relying on his knowledge as a novice. While serving as an apprentice under a master plumber, he was able to obtain new knowledge that enabled him to become a competent master plumber. I want you to give yourself permission to take on **new knowledge** and **new information**. Do not allow the knowledge and information you already have to restrict your growth. The knowledge you have is not all bad; it's just not enough to get you to your life's hopes and dreams.

There is an Old Persian proverb that goes, in part, as follows:

> He/she who knows not, and knows not that he/
> she knows not is a fool; shun them.
>
> He/she who knows not, and knows that he/she
> knows not, is ignorant; teach them.
>
> He/she who knows, and knows not that he/she
> knows is asleep; wake them.

Which of these descriptions best describes you? Are you a fool? Are you ignorant? Or, are you asleep? I believe that you know and know not that you know and this book is written to awaken you. If the knowledge you need was not already within you, you would have no reasonable basis for **hope**. Give yourself permission to reawaken the knowledge that is within you and to take on new knowledge and information that will help guide you to personal freedom.

1

FORMATION OF T1 THINKING

The term T1 Thinking refers to the first significant change in one's self concept. Children of all races, cultures, ethnic groups, rich or poor rely on their parents and other adult caretakers to form their self concept. Children are born with an innate ability to develop a healthy view of themselves and others. They hold their parents in high regard and look to them to provide a mirror of their self concept. When adult caretakers (who were also misinformed as children) unknowingly provide misinformation to their children, T1 Thinking is born in those children. This may occur as early as five years of age. T1Thinking represents powerfully negative thoughts about the self that are developed in early childhood and based upon **mis-information** received from **primary caretakers**. It is difficult for children to avoid internalizing the misperceptions of their parents and other adult caretakers. The negative experiences of children are real, but the child's interpretation of their negative experiences is not accurate. Children have 'clean hands' because they did nothing wrong. However, children born and/or raised in a T1 environment begin to form misperceptions of themselves and others. The child's misinterpretation of primary caretaker reactions is injurious to the child's view of him/herself and others. The injury to self is multi-faceted and can include injury to self identity; self satisfaction; behavioral self; moral self; personal self; family self; social self; and physical self. The combined effect of injuries to self renders the child's relationship with him /herself impaired. The injury to self will remain until the injury is reversed.

T1 adult caretaker reactions to children are manifested as emotional neglect, disparaging remarks, verbal abuse, emotional unavailability, low quality parent-child interaction, and other acts of commission or omission, which are internalized and become the children's view of themselves. Children experience negative adult caretaker reactions and immediately think they are the culprit. Children think that they are to blame for adult caretaker's negative reactions and negative behaviors. Children view themselves much like their caretakers perceive themselves.

The finest material goods that money can buy such as designer clothes; shoes; cars; fine schools; or world travel do not compensate or prevent children in T1 environments from forming misperceptions of themselves. Children don't need everything you can buy them; they need to know who they are. Children need at least one adult who can help them to accurately interpret the reactions of T1 adults in their lives in order to reduce injury to the self. Without at least one healthy thinking adult, the child's misperceptions and negative thoughts of him/herself set the stage for future self-destructive behaviors and T1relationships that last for decades. Obsession with these negative thoughts can cause a child to spiral downward into depression, eating disorders, emotional trauma and other severe behavioral problems.

It is very difficult for T1 parents and other adult care-takers, who are self absorbed in a struggle for their own spiritual, mental and emotional survival, to respond appropriately to the needs of children under their care. These T1 parents have been struggling for emotional survival most of their lives and were misinformed by their T1 parents. The moment T1 parents are born, their grandchildren become T1. T1 Thinking is instantly **trans-generational**. Therefore, we cannot blame parents who unknowingly experienced T1 Thinking and who simply did the best they could do to raise their children.

Some additional characteristics of T1 Thinking are:

» low self-concept;

» an innate and unconscious distrust of those of close kinship or relationship;

» an inability to develop and maintain intimate relationships;

» a resume of unsatisfying dating or marital relationships;

» a need to wear a 'mask' to control the thoughts of others;

» drama filled relationships with significant others;

» a need to be on constant guard from emotional assault;

- frequent feelings of anxiety;
- history of substance abuse and other self-destructive behaviors; and
- the inability to answer the question, **who am I**?

T1 Thinking is not healthy and it is uncommon to find a T1 Thinking person in a close relationship with a healthy thinking person. T1 relationships obstruct emotional wellness for all people involved. Healthy relationships are not perfect, yet they promote emotional wellness of all people involved.

People with T1 Thinking tend to form close relationships with others who also have T1 Thinking. A person might work every day; pay bills on time; and maintain a well kept home; yet, routinely find him/herself in a relationship that does not represent their best interest. T1 Thinking seems 'normal' since most of the people they know think that way. This is how T1 networks are formed. A **T1 Network** is the broader group of family members, significant others, and associates with whom T1relationships are maintained. A typical T1 network may begin at a point in time between 2 adults who were raised in T1 families. These individuals are involved in what they perceive to be a healthy relationship; but it is actually a T1 relationship. Both individuals are driven to each other by natural human needs. However, their T1 Thinking causes misperception of themselves and each other. It prevents them from enjoying a productive and healthy union. They eventually decide to raise children who, by age 5, begin to develop T1 Thinking. When these children reach a certain age, they will begin to go out into the world and establish their own T1 networks. Their children's children (if not reversed) will be the next T1 generation.

T1 individuals' self-destructive thinking is compounded by members of their T1 network. Membership in T1 networks is important to T1 individuals. However, these interactions serve to reinforce self-destructive thinking. For instance, you find yourself with a cold, interacting with a person who has the flu. Somehow, you think that you are going to make each other better. One of you sneezes all day while the other coughs all day. A cold/flu relationship is not healthy.

It is understandable how T1 Thinking acts as cement to form strong negative bonds between well-meaning people. T1 Thinking and the T1 relationships they derive have become a virtual subculture within society. To members of this subculture, the entire society appears to have T1 Thinking and involvement in T1 relationships. Everyone lives this way.

You might ask the question, 'Can I recover'? Yes, because you are resilient. You are never too young or too old to begin to get better. You have the power to restore your own healthy thinking and to prevent T1 Thinking in future generations. You have the power, right now, to impact your great, great grand-children, and it starts here. It starts with you. It transfers from you to your children and their significant others. This powerful change in thinking travels from generation, to generation, to generation. You should be excited because you can do something that is life giving for yourself that will also impact those not yet born. Future generations will have no idea of the hard work you put into yourself to make their lives better than your own. You have to make the sacrifice, so they can be free.

One of the unique characteristics of T1 Thinking is that it does not impact Intelligence Quotient or IQ. Some individuals have well above average to high IQs **and** T1 Thinking. These persons may be professionals, leaders, politicians, actors, musicians, athletes, academics or IT gurus. However, T1 Thinking can affect Emotional Quotient (EQ). A good Emotional Quotient is important to success in life beyond intellectual fame and fortune. T1 Thinking can reduce your ability to be aware of, express, and manage your emotions. It reduces your capacity to manage interpersonal relationships in an effective and empathic manner. T1 Thinking can prevent you from understanding your own emotions and the emotions of others. Despite IQ level, individuals with T1 Thinking often do not have the emotional skill set (EQ) necessary to engage in healthy relationships with themselves and particularly others who are close and important to them. The relationships formed by individuals with T1 Thinking are called T1 relationships.

T1 RELATIONSHIPS

A guy came to my office one day requesting marital counseling. He spoke at length about the beauty of their marriage. He stated they only needed to iron out a few wrinkles and they would have a "banging" marriage. So I said, "If you have had this beautiful marriage for eight years, why were you unfaithful to her during the first few months, and for years thereafter"? He responded, "Oh no"! I then asked, "Why is she staying at her mother's house, again, to be away from you?" I told him, "I am listening to you and I want to believe you, but what you say indicates that you actually have a T1 relationship".

A T1 relationship is a **collision** between two or more T1 individuals. Unlike unhealthy or toxic relationships, T1 relationships are characterized by injury to the **self** of all members of the T1 relationship. Those with an injury to the self tend to form negative bonds with others who have an injury to self. Those with an injury to self form T1 relationships with other T1 individuals who reflect negative attributes they already ascribe to themselves. All members of T1 relationships have injury to the self that is based in false perceptions and beliefs about themselves and others.

In T1 relationships, the only relationship that can be repaired is the individual's relationship with him/herself. Restoration of a healthy relationship with the self must take place before a healthy relationship with others can be developed. T1 relationships are an unconscious and futile attempt to repair the self via close relationships with other self injured individuals. This course of repair of self cannot be achieved. They subsequently blame each other for causing their **preexisting self** injuries. No one in T1 relationships is aware of the injury they have suffered to the self. The injury appears asymptomatic but it is clearly visible in one's negative view of him/herself and difficulty at forming healthy relationships with those who are important to them. This is why T1 relationships are characterized by **Drama!** T1 individuals spend decades attempting to form healthy relationships despite any evidence indicating their relationship will ever yield love, peace, and happiness for themselves and their significant others.

T1 relationships are **fatally flawed** because of injury to the self of all members of the relationship. Bandages may be applied, but the relationship(s) will always be T1. No matter what label you place on a T1 relationship such as marriage, husband, wife, etc., it will not change. For instance, let's say the car of your dreams is a Rolls Royce, but you can only afford a Hyundai. If you place a Rolls Royce emblem on a Hyundai, you still have a Hyundai. If you call a

T1 relationship a marriage, it is still a T1 relationship. Even though condonation, voluntary forgiveness for an offense, does not apply to T1 marriages, forgiveness is routinely given while both individuals in the T1 marriage continue to offend and re-injure each other. They find themselves on an emotional merry-go-round for years, looking for a way to get off. You cannot think of any other endeavor in your life wherein you would invest 20 years of time, energy, and/or money and receive little to no return on your investment. Would you place money in a savings account for 10 to 20 years while seeing your account balance diminish each month? Would you enroll in college and work hard for 20 years and still expect, but not yet have your undergraduate degree? Of course you would not do this. But T1 relationships get a **free pass**. You do not hold your T1 relationships to the same standards you use to measure other areas of your life.

Change starts with calling it what it is; a T1 relationship. When you repair your relationship with yourself, you will realize that you cannot have a healthy relationship with anyone who still has T1 Thinking, no matter how important they are to you. Let's say you want a healthy marital relationship. A healthy marital relationship is one wherein individuals can share genuine love and intimacy first with themselves, then with each other. **Love** is the ability to **first** give unconditional trust, intimacy, affection and support to yourself, then relate to others as you relate to yourself. **Intimacy** is the ability to share closeness and belonging with others. Intimacy is much more than sex. An intimate relationship may involve sharing of sex but it also includes effective communication, openness, reciprocity, trust and vulnerability. If you are a member of a T1 relationship, you may share sex with each other, but not other key components of intimacy.

Intimacy is not found in T1 relationships. Intimacy is a prerequisite for any close and healthy relationship between family members, friends, men, women and all people.

Mistrust is a characteristic of T1 relationships. Mistrust is actually a survival mechanism in T1 relationships. You are aware that you should not trust those who are close to you. Why? Because the people associated with your injured self were not strangers, but those who are close and important to you; fathers, mothers, grandfathers, step-fathers; uncles; older brothers; and cousins. You feel that it is only a matter of time that you will again be betrayed or disappointed. So, trust is a **guarded** trust. You trust in this way to protect yourself from inevitable harm to your **self**. Since you are invariably harmed despite your effort to protect yourself, the need to mistrust others is reinforced. Your trust in others is routinely misplaced. You repeatedly give trust to those important to you who simply cannot be trusted. Their record clearly demonstrates they cannot handle your trust, but you misplace your trust in them anyway. This is your way of unconsciously reinforcing your false believe that **people** cannot be trusted. The reality is that **people** you select to trust cannot be trusted.

In order to trust others, you must be able to trust yourself. The reason you don't trust you is because your own track record of poor judgment, poor decision-making and negative outcomes regarding important relationships, says you cannot trust yourself.

You must begin to **learn** how to trust yourself. You can start by trusting that you will not place yourself in harm's way. See the harm before it comes, and make sure you are not in its path. Learn how to take a step back when you are stressed and feel overwhelmed. If you are in stressful space, take yourself to a place where you can get five minutes of peace and quiet. You need to do that for you. Take a look at your **self**; take care of your **self**. You cannot expect another person to do for you, what you have not done for yourself. It is unreasonable to expect someone else to do for you, what you have not shown a willingness to do for yourself.

DRAMA IN T1 RELATIONSHIPS

Mistrust is also an underlying cause of **Drama** in T1 relationships. Drama is defined as intense verbal and sometimes physical interaction between T1 individuals. Criticisms, real or imagined, from those who are important to you produce drama. You feel chastised and as if you can never do anything right. You can't escape criticism whether it is expressed or silent. You may feel criticized by what is spoken or by what is unspoken.

Criticism is also an internal affair. What about the criticism you get from yourself? You would be surprised to discover how much T1 generated criticism you inflict upon yourself on a daily basis. When your own self criticism becomes overwhelming, you may begin to criticize others for relief. This is a double standard that says, 'It's ok for me to criticize me, but others cannot criticize me'. You must begin to hold yourself to the same standard you apply to others.

Drama is a result of unmet T1 **fantasy**. T1 fantasy is a process of creating **unrealistic** and improbable mental images based upon psychological needs. T1 individuals blame each other for not meeting each other's needs. You use fantasy to place titles on yourself and those important to you that are not substantive such as husband, wife, marriage, etc.

You use fantasy to place **false expectations** upon yourself and those important to you that **cannot** be met. The only way you can have the relationship you need psychologically is through T1 fantasy. This is a recipe for disaster. It is a circular and time consuming exercise in futility. You can spend years involved in fantasy driven drama in an attempt to get others to be what you need them to be. No one in T1 relationships realize they cannot share a healthy relationship with someone who has never experienced a healthy relationship. Over time, drama feels 'normal'. The more normal drama feels, the more difficult it becomes to let go. Drama is common in daily household interactions; at family functions; throughout the holidays; and especially at funerals. Drama provides all parties involved with a sense of control. During each episode of drama, all parties know what to say, how to feel, and how to act. Each episode is predictable, orchestrated, and everyone plays their unique roles. Drama takes on more unique characteristics with T1 couples. What drives T1 couples to maintain drama in their relationships?

YUV IN T1 RELATIONSHIPS

The primary rationalization T1 couples use for sharing drama is being in **YUV** (pronounced luv). **Yuv is a psychological defense used to justify behavior that would otherwise be insane**. The only way to prevent being committed to an inpatient psychiatric facility is to say, 'I Yuv him' or 'I Yuv her'. Once this word is uttered, the individual feels his/her insane behavior is justified. This is why you accept verbal and emotional abuse for years. This is why a man dove onto a speeding car and clutched the hood of the car while looking at his girlfriend through the windshield. The car reached speeds of over 80 mph before it was pulled over by police. After the police officer pried his fingers from the hood of the car, the man said he did it because he 'Yuvs her'. What is Yuv? It is a form of insanity. Individuals involved in T1 relationships think Yuv is love. They are unfamiliar with love. **Love** is the ability to give unconditional trust, intimacy, affection, and support to **oneself,** and then relate to others as you relate to yourself. Love neither looks, feels, nor behaves like Yuv. Love is like a Rolex watch; if your watch ticks, it's not a Rolex.

Now that you know what Yuv is, you have a responsibility to yourself to begin to reduce your participation in drama. The next time you are presented with an opportunity to participate in drama, think first. Your thinking must be based in reality. The reality is that you are in a T1 relationship. The relationship is flawed and cannot be repaired. Your most prudent recourse is to begin to change your relationship with you. Your relationship with you has beenT1. As your relationship with yourself improves, your ability to communicate; to effectively identify and solve problems; to avoid emotional traps; and to avoid drama will also improve.

FEAR AND PHOBIA

People involved in T1 relationships misuse the term fear. This misuse acts like cement and keeps participants bonded to each other. This cement represents how afraid you are to reduce your participation in the relationship. You convince yourself that if you leave the T1 relationship, you will be alone; no one else will want you; people will talk about you; your partner will find someone else to yuv; and you will be miserable for the rest of your life. This emotion is not fear. **Fear** is an unpleasant and often strong emotion caused by the anticipation or awareness of **real** danger. You cannot experience fear when the danger is not real. If you are at a shopping mall and you hear gunshots, you have every reason to fear. You can use the word fear when you are in a situation that requires notification of the police department, the fire department, or a priest. If any of these are not required, what you are feeling is phobia.

Phobia is an exaggerated and **illogical** fear of a particular situation. Phobia feels the same as fear, except that fear is based in **reality**, whereas phobia is based in one's **perception**. Phobia is a powerful emotion and sends many people to the emergency room complaining of a heart attack. Phobia is not real. Therefore, you don't have to be afraid to reduce your participation in T1 relationships. Your partner and others important to you do not keep you connected to T1 relationships; your own phobia does. You do not genuinely want to leave and the misuse of the word 'fear' allows you to justify staying in a stressful situation. Your determination to stay connected to T1 relationships reflects unresolved feelings of abandonment, rejection, and feelings of not having control from your childhood. It has little to do with your present T1 relationship. You have carried these intense feelings with you for years and unknowingly transferred them to T1 individuals who are currently important to you. These T1 individuals are strong representations of past important, yet disappointing relationships. So, you unconsciously use your present T1 relationships in a vain attempt to resolve issues that began in your childhood.

Misinformation plays a prominent role in phobia. Someone misinformed you that who you are holding onto; who you are clutching; is exactly who you think they are. But they're not. You came to believe that your T1 relationship has unlimited potential for success. You are willing to fight for this relationship because you are so afraid of losing what others told you that you have, or what you told yourself you have. You are also afraid of finding out that you may be wrong. You are afraid that you may have to start all over again. You are afraid of being alone. Guess what; you are already alone. You do not have to allow phobia to keep you this way. Phobia serves as an invisible prison and impedes your growth. You frighten yourself into paralysis and inaction because of phobia. Phobia is not good self-care. You do not have to allow phobia to keep you from moving forward; from getting to where you deserve to be in life. Now that you are aware, you can stop inappropriately using the word fear; just say, 'I am phobic about that'. The moment you hear yourself say the word phobic, you instantly know that your feelings are not reality based. You can acknowledge your feelings and just allow them to be; but you no longer have to panic and feel you must do something about your feelings. You are never obligated to respond to phobia because it is not real. You can spend less time feeling phobia and more time feeling that it is ok for you to be the best you can be.

KNOWLEDGE IN T1 RELATIONSHIPS

Knowledge of a condition or problem is handled differently by those in T1 relationships. These persons do not believe they have to change if they can show knowledge and awareness of a problem. This is done by simply saying, 'I know that...' regarding any negative situation brought to their attention. For instance, you may be asked if you are aware of your children's disruptive behavior at school. You may say, 'I know that'. Another question asked might be, 'Are you aware that your partner is considering calling 911 the next time you resort to violence? You may again reply, 'I know that'. What if someone told you that your 12 year old son is extremely disrespectful to his grandmother? You may respond, 'I know that'. Simply knowing about a problem does not absolve a T1 Thinking person of any further duty or obligation.

Intellect is the power of knowing. However, the power of knowing is different from the power to believe and the power of will. Just because you know something does not mean that you have the power to believe it or the will to carry it out. Therefore, T1 Thinking persons are more likely to get stuck on what they know. Despite a wealth of knowledge about the gravity of the situation, there is little meaningful change. Knowledge is not transferred down to believing what you know and to the will to act upon what you know. What you know should transfer to what you believe; what you believe becomes your will to do something about it. What you know, you also believe; and what you believe, you have the will to carry out. All three components must be connected and processed. This disconnect in T1 relationships happens because these individuals do not have a healthy belief or positive will. T1 relationships are based upon false knowledge; false belief; and negative will. False knowledge does not transfer to healthy belief or positive will. This is why you remain stuck despite your knowledge of deteriorating conditions in your T1 relationship. For now, know that healthy knowledge transfers to healthy belief. This belief transfers to positive will to carry out what you know and believe. This is a skill that must be developed over time. It is important for you to hold yourself accountable for assimilating the new knowledge you are learning; believing this new knowledge; and putting what you **know** and **believe** into **action** in your life.

SURVIVAL IN T1 RELATIONSHIPS

T1 relationships usually do not end abruptly. Once you learn that you are in a T1 relationship, it is usually more prudent to stay than leave immediately. If you leave immediately, you will only change your address, not your thinking. A change in thinking is the best way to resolve T1 relationships. You must discover and know, for **yourself**, that T1 relationships do not represent your best interest and that it is the right time for you to disengage. However, you should seriously consider leaving as soon as possible where there is a clear and present threat of physical harm or danger within the relationship.

Individuals involved in T1 relationships are usually found to be in one of three stages:

» Just coming out of a T1 relationship;

» Currently participating in a T1 relationship;
or

» Preparing to sign-up for another tour in a new T1 relationship with a new mate.

The term **mate** should be used when referring to T1 couples as opposed to wife, husband, spouse, fiancé, partner, etc. A mate is one of a matched pair. The key element that matches mates in T1 relationships is their T1 Thinking. But for their matched thinking, they would not be in a T1 relationship with each other.

At any stage, surviving in a T1 relationship is like being a passenger on the Titanic while trying to convince yourself that your ship is not sinking. You and your mate go to work every day and return home. You eat at the same table and you may still sleep in the same bedroom. You periodically attend various functions together. These activities help convince others, who don't live with you, that your relationship is 'normal'. You are just like they are, 'normal'. If you can convince other people that your relationship is 'ok', it is easier for you to believe that you are 'ok' and that your relation-**Ship**, the Titanic, is not sinking. Let's take a moment to assess whether your relationShip is sinking. Read each statement on the following questionnaire and circle your response. Give each statement **serious** consideration. You can easily score your questionnaire upon completion to determine the buoyancy of your relationShip.

Is My RelationShip Sinking Questionnaire

Please rate the following as it reflects your opinion of your mate (1 is low and 5 is high)

1.	EFFECTIVE COMMUNICATOR	1	2	3	4	5
2.	ABILITY TO LISTEN	1	2	3	4	5
3.	TRUSTWORTHINESS	1	2	3	4	5
4.	DEPENDABILITY	1	2	3	4	5
5.	ABILITY TO LOVE ME	1	2	3	4	5
6.	ABILITY TO RECEIVE LOVE	1	2	3	4	5
7.	ABILITY TO FULFILL ROLE IN RELATIONSHIP	1	2	3	4	5
8.	ABILITY TO FULFILL ROLE OF PARENT	1	2	3	4	5
9.	ABILITY TO MEET MY EXPECTATIONS	1	2	3	4	5
10.	OVERALL SATISFACTION WITH THE RELATIONSHIP	1	2	3	4	5

Score________

50 points is maximum score.
A minimum score of 35 is required for healthy relationship.
A score of less than 35 points is a sinking relationShip.

If your score indicates that your T1 relationShip is sinking, you will most likely continue in your relationShip. Let's take a look at several reasons why you are likely to continue:

1. T1 relationships serve as a balm to soothe emotional pain and 'fear'. The balm of T1 relationships offers temporary relief from loneliness, between episodes of drama.

2. You also stay because you convince yourself that you can 'help' your mate. You think that you have discovered the magic words or love potion that will cause your mate to blossom as never before. You think that you can be exactly who and what your mate needs in order to be happy and to make you happy. You change your appearance; take on a second job to bring in more money; graduate culinary school to improve your work in the kitchen; schedule vacations in the Caribbean and abroad; all to no avail. Ask yourself, what great changes have your mate achieved as a result of your 'help'?

3. One of the most prominent reasons for staying aboard a sinking relationShip is to keep your focus away from you and on your mate. Here is the beginning of a few sentences you may have used when you are upset with your mate:

    » You're this...
    » You're that...
    » If you would just...

» You always...
» You never...

You would rather spend 5 years or more criticizing your mate than 5 minutes in a mirror looking at the only person in the world you can change. You must come to accept that you cannot change your mate. Your mate may be satisfied with him/herself. There is an inverse relationship between satisfaction and change. The more satisfied a person is with him/herself, the less likely he or she will change. Are you willing to change without your mate? This is an important question for you to think about. Are you willing to place your destiny in the hands of someone else who shows little desire to be the best they can be? You are responsible for your own growth; change; and ensuring that you become the best you can be. No one else can accomplish this task for you. You can take the energy and effort that you waste trying to change others and invest it in making real change in yourself.

4. Low self-esteem is an unspoken reason for staying aboard a sinking relationShip. Low self-esteem is actually an insult to the self. It is an affront to the essence of your very being. Low self-esteem is a part of you that says 'I'm not good enough and I deserve to drown. No one will care'. Learn to be patient with yourself and don't write yourself off so quickly. Low self-esteem is often based upon mis-information that was incorporated into your self-perception when you were a child. As long as you hold on to this mis-information, you will experience low self-esteem. You really feel low

about yourself at times but the reality is your self-worth is much higher than you feel. You do not have to continue to allow low self-esteem to cause you to exist in T1 relationships.

5. Security is a reason that is often used to stay aboard a sinking relationShip. Individuals involved in T1 relationships are unconsciously aware of the emotional challenges they face. You feel fortunate to have found 'someone' who will accept you. Your mate feels the same way. There is a degree of security in knowing that you are not likely to leave each other for someone else because of your emotional **deficiencies**. You can stay in the relationship and avoid rejection which is sure to come from others. The proverb 'A bird in hand is worth two in the bush' is applied in T1 relationships. The thinking is that it is better to have a lesser mate than to risk the possibility of having a better person and end up with no mate at all. The innate human need for security prolongs T1 relationships. You are actually in an insecure situation that you think is secure. You can unknowingly remain is this fragile relationship for many, many years.

Regardless of how long you have been or will continue to be in your T1 relationship, you should not be idle. There are some positive steps you can start to take today. Remember, change is not about repairing your T1 relationship; change is about repairing you. Once your relationship with yourself is repaired and healthy, you can do what you choose about your T1 relationships.

1. It is critical that you make changing your T1 Thinking a top priority. Your thinking is under assault 24 hours per day. It is likely that you may need a combination of self-help groups such as AA, OA, NA, ALANON, grief, or other support groups; professional support; and/or spiritual support. You may be very bright, resourceful and/or successful, but you will not be able to single-handedly change your T1 Thinking.

2. Stop blaming your mate for being the source of your frustrations, disappointment, and unhappiness. Your mate was misinformed just as you were misinformed. As you continue to learn that T1 relationships are fatally flawed, you have an obligation to yourself to stop blaming and pointing fingers at your mate. Remember, if you point one finger at your mate, there are at least three fingers on your hand pointing back at you. Blaming your mate only reinforces your T1 Thinking. Focus on those three fingers and not the one pointing towards your mate. What three areas of change, needed in you, do your fingers represent?

3. Limit your discussions with your mate, as much as possible, to simple activities of daily living. Always strive to be civil and respectful

to your mate. You can place all other matters on 'hold' until you can reduce your own T1 Thinking.

4. Avoid discussion of highly charged emotional issues. This can be difficult since the slightest issue can become highly charged. If you find yourself in an emotionally charged discussion, just stop and remind yourself that the issue is not really about you and tell your mate that you do not want to participate in a discussion that is based on childhood misperceptions.

5. Journal about your emotions. Use old fashion pen and paper rather than typing via your computer.

6. Avoid getting enmeshed in conflict involving your family members; your mate's family members; or other relatives and/or associates. It is important not to allow yourself to be drawn in to conflict with members of your T1 network.

7. Listening to members of your T1 network while they share their T1 thoughts with you over the telephone reinforces their T1 Thinking. When you set aside an hour or more to listen to their misperceptions, you are co-signing their T1 Thinking. If their thinking is not valid, why would you waist

an hour or more listening to them? Begin to make yourself less available for entertaining other people's T1 Thinking.

8. Resist the false belief that you can actually sit down and reason with your T1 mate to resolve deep-seated conflict and differences. You have not been able to do so and you cannot do so now. Your attempt to resolve volatile emotional issues is a vain effort to convince yourself that you can stop your relationShip from sinking. Like the Titanic, it will sink.

9. Remind yourself daily that your mate cannot meet and is not responsible for meeting your lifelong unmet needs. Even if this was possible, you are responsible for learning how to meet your own needs.

   Let's point out a few other strategies that may help you endure T1 relationships while you work on changing the way you think. You do not have to accept some of your mate's behavior. Acceptance means to give approval and to endure something without protest. No one person is required or should give approval to insanity or endure insanity without protest. You should protest information and behavior from your mate that does not make good sense. For instance, your mate may insist that you follow their leadership on matters affecting the family such as parenting styles or finances. If your mate's track record in these areas has already crashed and burned, you have a duty to yourself and your children to protest and to exercise prudence. Moreover, you should protest against yourself for convincing you to place and keep yourself in this tenuous situation. You should not accept anyone's living beneath their privilege; this includes you. If someone has cancer, spinal bifida, Crohn's disease, etc., that is different; but T1 adults who are emotionally immature and satisfied with their T1 Thinking are not acceptable. You can acknowledge or take notice of your mate's T1 Thinking by saying, 'I take notice of what you do, but I do not accept your behavior'. In the interim, you are responsible for changing your own T1 Thinking which is the source of your contribution to the problems in all relationships with people who are close and important to you.

2

T2 THINKING

T2 Thinking represents the second major shift in one's misperception of him/herself. Those who develop T2 thinking pursue drugs, alcohol, food, gambling and other addictive behaviors (in part) to escape and/or to manage the powerfully negative emotions generated by their T1 Thinking. T2 individuals attempt to medicate (soothe) their emotions via the abuse of chemicals and other addictive behaviors. These behaviors are also unconsciously used to validate one's T1 Thinking and negative perceptions of the self. When a child, by age 12, becomes convinced that he/she is worthless, unloved, and rejected by primary caretakers, the abuse of drugs and alcohol begins to make sense. The adverse legal, physical, social, and financial problems that stem from substance use also serve to prove their unworthiness and validate their self rejection. Self loathing dominates one's negative thinking. Drugs and alcohol provide temporary relief from the emotional anguish caused by feelings of lifelong rejection and not fitting in. Drugs and alcohol become a primary coping mechanism for children who have been sexually molested by their relatives or persons 'close' to the family. In such cases, T1 Thinking can develop as a result of the molestation. T1 Thinking predisposes many, but not all, to T2 Thinking and its various addictive behaviors.

T2 Thinking can lead to 20 or more years of substance abuse. When you are able develop to a pattern of abstinence, you are **sober**. In other words, your body is no longer under the influence of an external substance used to alter your thoughts and emotions. When a T2 person becomes sober, he/she immediately returns to their prior state of T1 Thinking, which has continued to progress. The only problems that are solved when you get sober are some of the problems caused by your substance abuse. Simply getting sober does not automatically solve other major problems related to your T1 Thinking or your emotional maturity (EQ). Once sober, you quickly return to T1 Thinking because it never went away. You may be sober for 20 years and relapse into substance abuse because T1 Thinking continues after the addictive behavior stops. Let's look at it this way. There are two types of alcoholics: alcoholics who drink (T2) and alcoholics who don't drink (T1). Alcoholism is not only about how much a person drinks; it's also about how one thinks. In order to be an alcoholic, all you have to do is think like one. Alcoholic thinking is self-destructive. T1 thinking is equally self-destructive; it just does not involve the consumption of alcohol.

When you get sober, T2 changes to T1 and there is a tendency to relax. You no longer wake up in strange places and with people you don't even know. You don't drive under the influence and land yourself in jail anymore. However, you are still a thinking addict (T1). As long as you think like an addict, you will be an addict and at risk for relapse into addictive behaviors. That's why, for many, recovery is a lifelong process. Why? Because you think this way for the rest of your life. The fundamental T1 Thinking that predisposed you to addiction has not changed since you were 5 or 6 years old. When a person gets sober and spends years **not** working to change his/her T1 Thinking, this is commonly referred to as being a 'dry drunk'. T1 Thinking distorts information and hampers emotional growth. You don't get what is actually being communicated and don't know that you don't get it. Working to reduce your T1 Thinking after getting sober will prevent you from living your life stuck on sober.

STUCK ON SOBER

T1 Thinking masks important issues that do not receive enough attention after you get sober and keeps you at risk for relapse into T2 Thinking and its addictive behaviors. Some of the issues that are common to those stuck on sober include: abandonment; low self-esteem; feeling unloved; T1 relationships; self-criticism; low EQ; **secrets**; guilt; and shame.

These issues can be very painful and embarrassing. They are worsened due to your daily interactions with members of your T1 network. The last things you want to talk about when you get sober are these painful and embarrassing issues. Moreover, people close to you in your T1 network pose a threat to your recovery as they unknowingly reinforce your T1 Thinking. T1 individuals do not know who they are. People who don't know themselves cannot affirm who you are.

The first order of business is finding out who you are. You ought to know who you are before you get out of bed every morning. If you don't know who you are, it is very easy to get lost. You will need appropriate recovery supports and resources in order to overcome your T1 thinking and move from living sober, to living in sobriety.

Sobriety reflects the quality of your thinking and emotions. Sobriety of thought automatically produces sobriety of emotion. Sobriety of thought is a requirement for a healthy EQ or emotional maturity. Healthy people have quality sobriety. Sobriety is when at least 7 out of 10 of your thoughts and emotions are consistently positive, constructive, and productive for you. This is called the **'70% test'**. Sobriety allows you to be at peace with yourself and others who live in sobriety. It is important to remember that **sober** and **sobriety** are **not** interchangeable terms. This is why those in recovery might have 20 years sober and 2 years sobriety. These timelines are never equal and sober years will exceed the number of years in sobriety. You are not required to wander aimlessly for 40 years in the land of sober. The great news about getting sober is that it affords you an opportunity to begin to develop a quality sobriety. This process involves replacing misinformation with new information. This new information changes the way you think about yourself and others. T1Thinking has been the source of the problems and sobriety means T1 Thinking has been significantly reduced. It can be very difficult to discard misinformation about yourself, especially when you have relied upon it for so long. Now is the time to reassess and reevaluate what you have 'known' for years. Where you find knowledge to be incorrect and self-defeating, discard it. Open your mind and begin to develop a quality sobriety, which is equal to healthy thinking. Everyone can and deserves an opportunity to live in sobriety.

3

DENIAL IN T1 RELATIONSHIPS

Denial is a formidable obstacle that keeps you connected toT1 relationships. Denial is commonly found in T1 relationships. According to the Big Book dictionary, "denial is a psychological defense mechanism in which confrontation with a personal problem or reality is avoided by refusing to accept the existence, truth, or validity of the problem." Denial prevents you from realizing that your relationships with those important to you are T1. All warnings signs that clearly identify your relationships as T1 are rendered invisible to you by denial.

Imagine a lady who wants to form a 2-person co-ed basketball team. She sets up and holds tryouts to identify a male partner for her team. She carefully questions a male candidate about his basketball experience, ball handling skills, dribbling skills and shooting skills. The male candidate proudly discusses his skill in all of these areas. Upon completion of her interview, she selects the man to join her team, despite the fact that the man has no arms. The man with no arms also ignored the obvious and went along with her in order to make her team. She became angry with him at their first game when he dropped every ball passed to him; he could not dribble the ball; and he had difficulty shooting the ball. As the season progressed, she became more critical of him and disappointed in him because of their losing record. However, she never asked herself how this man ever got on her team. It should be noted that no talented male basketball players were ever interviewed to be her teammate. No talented male candidates were considered by her.

This is denial at work in a T1 relationship. You are not able to see that you picked your partner for your team. You are not able to see that the person you picked was 'disabled' from the beginning and he/she was not capable of fulfilling your expectations as a partner. Denial prevents you from realizing this person never had what you needed, but you said that he/she met your qualifications and blamed them for agreeing with you. Denial prevents you from realizing that just because you say it, doesn't make it so. Denial causes you to see what you **need** to see in people important to you. Denial prevents you from seeing who people important to you **think** they are.

Titles such as husband and father indicate denial in T1 relationships. Simply giving someone a title does not make it so. If a man does not currently meet or exceed the requirements of being a competent husband or father, then he is a husband or father in title only. Roles in T1 relationships are no more than ceremonial or biological titles. Husbands and fathers in healthy relationships consistently meet or exceed the expectations of their roles and responsibilities. If you believe that you are in a relationship with a husband, father, mother, partner or other close relationship, take a moment to assess whether or not these individuals consistently meet or exceed their responsibilities in the relationship. If necessary, speak to someone who is knowledgeable, competent and not connected to your T1 social network. This may be a preferred option because you should not ask anyone who is in denial, even yourself, for their opinion.

People involved in various T1 relationships are driven by natural emotional needs. They are driven by a need for love, intimacy, safety and protection. Denial, however, causes you to attempt to meet these needs in a self-destructive manner. You are spiritually, mentally and/or emotionally diminished in the process. For instance, devotion is a desirable attribute in a relationship. While in denial, devotion can be manifested in the form of secrets and lies. A T1 adult believes she is devoted to her husband by never telling anyone that he is verbally abusive and emotionally unavailable. If anyone gets suspicious and questions her, she may lie to protect him. Denial allows her to go about her daily activities for years as though none of this is taking place in her home life. Denial can lead to lifelong emotional devastation.

Denial can cause an illogical belief and unreasonable trust in yourself. Adults with T1 Thinking often want to lead their mates and family and they want the family to follow them. Denial prevents these individuals from asking the question, 'am I qualified to lead'? It prevents you from realizing that your inability to lead is why your mate and family are unwilling to follow. Denial prevents you from realizing you don't lead simply because, for instance, you are head of household; you lead because you consistently demonstrate an ability to do so. The family then feels safe knowing you're in charge, out front and capable of leadership. Denial causes T1 Thinking adults to be blind to this fact. The more you try and fail, the more effort you place into succeeding. Little or no effort is placed on reducing and eliminating denial which prevents you from developing effective leadership skills.

Denial is cunning and baffling. It causes a number of false feelings that include safety; comfort; security; control; solutions to problems; and ability to lead a 'normal' lifestyle. All of these feeling are false in denial. Individuals experiencing denial don't know it; they are unlikely to find out on their own; they may become angry if their denial is confronted; and they may become aware of denial only when problems produce overwhelming adverse consequences.

Since you have been misinformed from an early age, denial has become part of your identity. You have been unknowingly misinformed by people who are very important to you. As a result of internalizing years of misinformation, you identify yourself as unworthy; unwanted; broken; not belonging; insecure; unattractive; and an outcast. Denial causes you to refuse to accept the reality that you have been misinformed and to hold strongly to a fragile false identity.

Denial can also adversely impact your spiritual identity. Your identity (who you are) is directly connected to your Creator. You were actually born millions of years ago when your Creator **thought** of you. Your Creator cannot make a mistake; therefore, you are not a mistake. Your true identity can only come from your Creator. On a certain date during the 21st century, your Creator's thought of you was physically manifested into your present being. You refer to this event as your birthday. Since your birth date, your self-identity has changed. You identified yourself with the negative thoughts and misperceptions of your T1 caretakers. Your Creator has given **you** power. No person has power to define you, except that you give them power. The more you unknowingly give power to others to define you, the more you see them as **mini gods** whom you feel obligated to obey. Remember, your Creator's opinion and definition of you remains unchanged.

The extent to which you can identify with your Creator is the extent to which you can identify with your true identity.

You have embarked upon a journey to recover your true identity. This journey requires you to reconnect and to strengthen your **relationship** with your Creator. Devote a portion of each day (through study, prayer and meditation) to rediscover your Creator's definition of who you are. When you realign yourself with your Creator's definition, your life will begin to take on new purpose and new meaning.

4

COMMUNICATION IN T1 RELATIONSHIPS

Communication is essential to healthy relationships. Communication is used to express ideas and opinions; to share feelings; and to provide information. All members of healthy relationships are kept apprised, informed, and aware of pertinent issues and activities concerning their interactions. It is rare to find members of a healthy relationship in the dark regarding pertinent information. Members of healthy relationships are skilled at providing clear information and they are equally skilled at listening to each other. The ability to listen is critical to healthy communication.

Communication in T1 relationships operates by a different set of rules. Information is guarded; it is given out in small bits and pieces, over time; it is withheld; or it is left unspoken. Communication in T1 relationships often results in arguments, finger pointing, and confusion for all involved. The more T1 individuals speak the more the stories and information changes. This is because there is an inherent belief that what is being said or heard cannot be trusted. Adults and children in T1 relationships have been misled, disappointed, and heart-broken for years. These persons exercise control and protection from further harm by presenting information as a constantly moving target. In this manner, promises can go un-kept. Commitments can be more easily broken. Disavowal of information can help avoid responsibility. So, in T1 relationships, nothing gets done; no one is responsible; and no one knows about it. This is how innocent children in T1 relationships get left waiting at school for hours for the adult care-taker who forgot to pick them up; children of separated parents are saddened when their parent no longer living with them does not show up again to pick them up for the weekend; and two adults, living in the same house, cannot synchronize their schedule of activities on a daily basis to help the household activities operate more smoothly.

Individuals in T1 relationships often attempt to talk over or louder than one another. Listening is rare. The person, who is not speaking and appears to be listening, is merely waiting for the other person to take a breath and stop speaking. Communication is also difficult because the parties don't know themselves or each other. It is difficult to communicate effectively with a stranger.

There are several prominent dysfunctional communication types in T1 relationships. First, there is the **Vague** communicator. These individuals love to talk, but they are unclear and difficult to understand. Thoughts are disjointed and the ideas expressed are in disarray. You can listen to this person for an hour or more and have no clue as to what they're talking about. They just seem to ramble on and on without end.

The **Non-Expressive** communicator is one who prefers to stay at home in their favorite chair, looking at the newspaper; watching television; listening to jazz; and otherwise busy at remaining distant. It is always difficult to know if this person is well, sick, happy or sad because communication with anyone in the household is rare; but everyone knows to respect the person's space and to maintain a safe distance from them.

The **Double-Talker** is one who shares specific, detailed information. Five minutes later, this person adamantly denies any knowledge of what was clearly said moments earlier. This person did not say it or is always misunderstood by everyone.

The **Osmotic** communicator takes communication to another level. This person is capable of holding a two-way conversation about another person, without the other person's knowledge or presence. Imagine a man who gets up on Sunday morning and initiates an Osmotic (silent) conversation in the bedroom with his spouse who is outside working in the garden. He says that he will make his home group meeting; she will cook breakfast while he is gone to save time; after cooking breakfast, she will go to Jim's house to get their tickets for the ballgame. When he gets home, they can eat; he can get dressed; and they are out the door. Through osmosis, he asks his spouse if this plan is okay with her. Unbeknownst to his spouse, who is in their back yard, the answer is yes. The man makes his meeting, returns home and becomes angry and argumentative with his spouse, who has done none of what she unknowingly had agreed to do. He will never be convinced that the conversation never happened. He believes his spouse knew or should have known what he wanted her to do. Sound familiar?

The **High-Jacker** starts by talking about something that seems benign and legitimate, just to get you into a conversation; to get you to relax; and to believe that a fruitful discussion is about to take place. For instance, the conversation starts with a discussion of ways to improve family finances. Suddenly, the conversation takes a radical turn and shifts to 15 years ago and you are accused of taking $50 from his wallet while he was intoxicated. He exclaims that if his spouse had not taken the $50 from his wallet 15 years ago, they would not be in their poor financial situation today. This person will use any opportunity to resurrect and rehash old resentments that are irrelevant and imagined events.

Finally, there is the **Angry-Man** communicator who maintains an angry scowl on his face. He sends a clear message to others that says, don't talk to me; don't get close to me; don't approach me. His expression is visible from across the room. He is only approached when others have no other choice and he must be approached. You get in and out as quickly as you can with him. The Angry-Man found out that if he presents himself this way, he does not have to expose the fact that he is uncomfortable around people (particularly his own family) and that he feels very insecure at interacting with people. He has figured out that if he wears this 'angry mask' and cause people to believe the mask is actually real, he will not have to communicate. The Angry-Man communicator can hide behind his mask for 30 to 40 years in his own self-imposed prison.

Now, let's look at critical communication that is routinely by-passed in T1 relationships, particularly at the beginning and during the early stages of T1 couple relationships.

The honeymoon phase of new T1 relationships excludes real communication and information sharing. The honeymoon phase is a brief period of pseudo-harmony and goodwill. The honeymoon phase is when pent-up fantasies about being accepted and loved unconditionally by another person are unleashed. These fantasies are reinforced by other couples you see and **presume** to be happy together; romantic movies; or your favorite romance novels. You are quickly convinced, during the honeymoon phase, that your relationship troubles are in the past; the emotional pain is gone, and you feel terrific. It is like being on an emotional high. After a few weeks or months, the honeymoon phase ends. The emotional pain has increased and you begin to feel worse than you did before the new T1 relationship began. So, you try harder and harder to get your mate to change back to the loving, caring person you convinced yourself that you saw during the honeymoon. These efforts are to no avail because the relationship is T1.

At the beginning of T1 relationships, there is little or no communication regarding the absence of a successful history of relationships. If you date a person who has virtually no history of positive, successful relationships, why do you think it will be different this time? If a person wants to work for you and the person has no positive, successful work history, would you consider the person to be a good candidate for hire? The absence of prior success in relationships is down-played and is not a conversational priority to T1 couples.

There is little conversation and inquiry with individuals who have had multiple relationships, multiple marriages that all ended negatively. When this information is apparent, why would you say, I want to be next? These are red flags that should generate conversation and discussion. These red flags say, keep out; stay away; do not enter; yet, you walk right in and often without hesitation.

There is no conversation about the person's history of emotional problems, turmoil, and drama within their family of origin. When you meet the person's family and mental/emotional problems become apparent within the first 5 minutes, remember this person is a product of that tumultuous environment. Trees have been known by the fruit they bare. T1 couples do not recognize the red flags made clearly visible by information about each other's family of origin.

There is also little conversation between T1 couples around their blended children. When it is known that their children are experiencing behavioral and academic problems, this can be a red-flag. While children are not to blame, there must be some concern and discussion of the person's parenting skills, availability and interaction with their children. Children serve as 'canaries in a coal mine' regarding the overall health of the family. Children suffering with ADD; ADHD; depression; eating disorders; and substance abuse are often responding to the lack of quality of interaction and care provided by their adult caretakers. If the children are not well, a red-flag must go up and communication should take place with the adult care-taker regarding their role in the children's at-risk state of emotional and behavioral health.

While it may appear that T1 couples ignore communication in these critical areas, there is a basis for the apparent lack of communication on these subjects. Communication around these subjects take-on a different shape and meaning with T1 couples. Let's closely examine this apparent lack of communication. Although it is not openly and specifically discussed, T1 couples are keenly aware of each other's disappointments in previous relationships; they are aware of each other's traumatic family history; and they are concerned about their children's emotional well-being. Nevertheless, the couple's T1 Thinking allows them to believe they are a perfect match for each other. Sharing similar family backgrounds and experiences allows them to feel more at ease and more comfortable with each other. These similarities also reduce the possibility of rejection. So, a history of broken relationships; being raised in a broken family; and current feelings of emotional distress are not viewed as red flags, but as common ground for mutual understanding by T1 couples. Although they are drawn to each other by legitimate human needs, T1 couples' denial prevents them from recognizing they are entering a T1relationship. All warning signs and red flags are rendered invisible by their denial. After a few days or weeks, T1 couples will fall in **Yuv** with each other and the stage is set for months or years of continued disappointment and despair.

There is one other form of communication that is unique in all T1 relationships. Every person involved in T1 relationships also has a T1 relationship with themselves. There is a negative and critical conversation taking place within you. This conversation with yourself is comprised of **T1 Thoughts**. These painful and shameful thoughts reflect your own self-criticism about your being over-weight; your below average appearance; your inability to fit-in; how you should be farther ahead in life than you are now; and the low opinion other people have of you. When no one else is present, this conversation takes place in your mind about you. These T1 thoughts also serve as the basis for your own self- abandonment; self rejection; and overall dislike of yourself. Statements such as 'I am not worth it,' 'I am not good enough' become the central theme of your conversation with yourself. These powerfully negative thoughts about you begin to color and shape your relationship with yourself and others. The criticism you accept from others begins to mirror your criticism of yourself. Because of the way you think about yourself, the criticism from others becomes tremendously painful. Your participation in T1 relationships becomes an outward reflection of your inner thoughts about you. The crux of your daily conversation with you is your deep abiding belief that you do not **deserve** to be treated with respect, love and admiration. This false belief is at the core of your T1 Thinking and drives your negative conversation with yourself. This conversation with yourself has been maintained in secrecy.

Now is the time for this ongoing secret conversation with you to be exposed to the light of truth. It is time to cease your negative conversation. It's time to begin to have a healthier conversation with yourself. Let's start by introducing new and more accurate information about you into your conversation. Imagine you having a conversation with you and about you. Speak to you as though you are beginning a new relationship with yourself. In order to develop your new relationship with you, there are several new healthy thoughts about you that are to be discussed and incorporated in the way you think about you. First, set aside any concerns; open your mind to the possibility of a new relationship; imagine you when you were 5 years old; and begin speaking slowly and directly to you as follows:

» It is now time for me to begin to recover, my personal freedom.

» I will learn how to give unconditional love to myself.

» I will not scare myself with phobic thoughts.

» I will not punish myself.

» I will not criticize myself.

» I don't need to be perfect.

» I deserve to treat me kindly.

» I deserve to treat myself with respect.

» I will do what is in my best interest.

» I will forgive myself.

» I am worth it.

» I am good enough.

» I love myself.

These statements are not mere affirmations. They are **mantras** that are repeated often as an expression of your new fundamental belief about you. They can be spoken directly to you out loud or as silent utterances in your thoughts. Select one mantra per day and spend five minutes to one hour or more per day repeating your selected mantra out loud or in meditation on your mantra. Overtime, these new healthy thoughts will begin to replace your T1 Thinking.

This exercise will help you begin to discover the importance of giving to yourself. You do have a self or 'Me' inside of you that needs and deserves your attention.

5

ME

This moment in your life is devoted to the 'Me' that lives silently, patiently and lovingly within you. Let's call this, 'Me' time. You have had a 'Me' inside of you since birth. The 'Me' inside you represents your original, genuine, unadulterated self. Despite everything you have gone through in life, the 'Me' in you has never changed. It is not possible to change the 'Me' in you from its original, untainted condition. At this moment, the 'Me' in you is intimate; trusting; loving; and at peace. The 'Me' in you has unconditional love for you and is always seeking happiness and wellbeing for you. The 'Me' in you is unwavering and, in the face of adversity, dependable and supportive of you. The 'Me' in you will not forsake you. The 'Me' in you is your best friend. Your life's hopes and dreams are embodied in the 'Me' in you. You cannot experience your hopes and dreams without the 'Me' in you.

While the 'Me' in you has not changed, your **perception** of the 'Me' inside you has undergone a significant change. Over the years, you have paid increasingly more attention to people around you and increasingly less attention to the 'Me' in you. Your perception of your 'Me' (or your Self) has been tarnished, initially by your T1 adult caretakers, and subsequently by other T1 people important to you. Your focus has undergone a significant shift from your original relationship with yourself, to your T1 relationship with others. When you disconnect from the 'Me' in you, you simultaneously disconnect with your being. Your original self, or your 5 year old, is neglected. You become consumed with the way other people see you; what other people think about you; with other people's problems; how to please and make other people happy; and how to keep people important to you from leaving your life. Your perception of you has become a reaction to the perception of people important to you. You have falsely believed that other people hold the key to your 'Me'. This is why you have spent years trying to get T1 individuals to give you what they do not have. For instance, when you meet someone and begin to form a new dating relationship, you can spend up to 40 hours per week interacting with them. You begin to invest enormous amounts of time into your relationship. You begin to have extensive telephone conversations. You begin to go to movies and restaurants with each other. You begin to have home visits and sleepovers. You begin to take weekend trips together and eventually, extended vacations. Your life becomes consumed with your new dating relationship. You refer to each other as a couple, albeit a T1 couple. You willingly spare no expense in getting your new relationship off the ground.

Now, ask yourself this question; 'how much time am I willing to invest in renewing my relationship with 'Me'? You are willing to work a new T1 relationship like a full-time job. Are you willing to invest that level of energy and effort in yourself? It is time to put 'Me' first. It is time to learn how to invest first in yourself by paying attention to your own spiritual, emotional and physical needs. These ingredients are essential to a healthy relationship with the 'Me' in you. Once you learn how to give to yourself, you will know how to give to others. You will also realize that you cannot have a healthy relationship with T1 individuals regardless of how important they are to you. A healthy 'self' cannot share healthy interactions with an 'injured self'. Once you reconnect with the 'Me' inside you, you can enjoy healthy relationships with others who have a healthy relationship with themselves. A healthy relationship with the 'Me' in you will guide the development of your relationships with others.

Relationship Formation: A Healthy Perspective

We have talked about T1 relationships. Now, let's take a moment to look at healthy relationships. This information is important to the healthy 'Me' in you. Healthy individuals develop relationships with others in several stages. Each stage is determined by the amount of factual, evidence-based information known about the person or persons. Each stage builds upon the previous stage, depending upon the content of additional information collected over time. The information collected in each stage dictates whether the relationship will remain at the present stage or proceed to the next stage. It is important to know as much as possible about the person before entering a relationship. Unfortunately, there are many who enter the relationship first, then begin to gather important information about the individual. By the time you find out, the damage is done. It is time to take better care of the 'Me' in you by adopting a healthier perspective on relationships.

The Acquaintance Stage:

As an adult, all new relationships begin as acquaintances. An acquaintance is an individual about whom you possess little knowledge and information. You may only know the person's name, rank, and serial number. You may encounter and speak with this person every day for a year at the bus stop, the supermarket, or at school. Yet, this person is an acquaintance because you have limited vital information about the person. You may notice that the person speaks well, seems very intelligent, appears polite, dresses well and is always well groomed. Your relationship with this person is an acquaintance relationship because of the shallow amount of information you possess. An acquaintance is one step above a stranger. Individuals with whom you have been acquainted for six months to a year should not have the keys to your home, the keys to your car or your telephone number. They should not have access to sensitive, personal identifying information about you. A majority of people you know are acquaintances regardless of the title you give them. An acquaintance relationship can evolve to the next stage when there is an absence of red flags or other behaviors observed during the acquaintance stage. Red flags consist of any information and/or behavior that would inform a reasonable person to limit their interaction to the acquaintance stage. For instance, a person showing any sign of T1 Thinking or T2 Thinking should automatically be restricted to the acquaintance stage. This is important because it is not uncommon for a T1 person to become emotionally devastated because an **acquaintance** did not seem interested enough in them to ask for their phone number or to ask for a date. A T1 person can easily become depressed because an **acquaintance** simply did not return a phone call or did not accept them as a 'friend' on a social website. This behavior is a major red flag. In the absence of red flags, you can openly discuss and mutually agree to begin a social relationship.

The Social Stage:

During this stage, you share social activities such as movies, sporting events, cultural events, and other activities that are mutually enjoyable. Moreover, social events provide additional opportunities to collect information about the individual. You can observe how the individual interacts under various social situations and circumstances. It is important to have fun, but it is equally important to gather information that will help you determine the appropriate stage of interaction with this individual. If information collected during the social stage says 'warning' or 'caution,' you cannot ignore the information. For T1 Thinking persons, warning or caution signs can become invisible. For instance, a T1 person may become extremely jealous if you decide to socialize with someone else. They become increasingly demanding of your time and attention. Some T1 persons may require a legal restraining order against them before they cease their harassment of you.

Your decision about the appropriate stage of your relationship is constantly informed by the evidence-based information you collect. Social relationships may last for years, as long as the information collected supports this decision. Information you collect should be able to stand on its own and it not be sanitized by you. Your decision making about your social relationship with the individual is driven by your evidence-based observations, not only by your emotional needs. Social relationships are the second largest group of interactions you will maintain. When there are no red flags, it is ok to give limited personal identifying information such as your address and phone number in order to promote the social relationship.

The Friendship Stage:

Friendship is a strong, intimate relationship between two or more healthy people. Friendship is a relationship often developed over a period of many years. A friendship allows you freedom to be your true self; freedom to express your true feelings; you are worthy of trust; you are free to be honest; you are secure enough to be vulnerable; you are free to be imperfect; and you are reliable and dependable. Friendship constantly seeks the best interest of all members of the relationship. The actual number of friends you have in life can be counted on one hand. Friends are few and far between. A friend serves as another set of eyes and ears for the 'Me' in you. A friend will not patronize you or seek advantage in a relationship with you. In order to have a friendship with another healthy person, you must have a healthy friendship with the 'Me' in you.

The term friendship is often misapplied to represent less significant forms of relationships. A friend is not simply someone with whom you have been associated for many years. T1 individuals misuse this term often. They consider themselves friends despite the drama, chaos and confusion they share on a regular basis. T1 friends are actually short or long-term T1 acquaintances or T1 social relationships. Those who are not friends first to themselves cannot be friends to others.

The Dating Stage:

Friendships may progress to the next stage of relationships which is the dating stage. A minimum of 1 to 2 years of data collection should be completed prior to entering the dating stage. This may include the time you have spent in the acquaintance and social stages of your relationship. During your friendship, you develop a wealth of information which may support a dating relationship. This period of time is not intended to be scientific. It is not intended to represent right or wrong. However, a minimum of 1 to 2 years of data collection represents the level of importance you place on your dating relationship. This relationship is not taken casually. It is just as important as purchasing a home. You take all the time you need, even 1 to 2 years, to collect information on the property and ensure that your home investment is solid and secure. Dating is an investment in the 'Me' in you. While dating, you continue to collect information about your partner. Time allows natural events, challenges, and hardships to unfold. You can assess the enduring strength of your bond. How does your relationship tolerate periods of highs and lows; feast and famine; or wealth and poverty? These experiences and events provide excellent feedback regarding the level of trust, intimacy, and love present in your dating relationship.

This is why it is important to take time to collect data on trust, intimacy, and love. The trend, however, has become to date first, and then collect information. Moreover, the popular trend is to speed date, have children, get married and then collect information about the relationship. If you have attempted this method, how successful has it been for you? Do you treat other important areas of your life this way? For instance, would you accept a job without first getting information about the job duties and salary? Would you consent for surgery without first getting information about the doctor and his/her surgical skills at the type of surgery you need? Of course you would not; you deserve the same consideration in your dating relationships. A healthy dating relationship requires you to take time to develop the trust, the intimacy, and the love.

Trust provides reasonable comfort and security in knowing that your emotional and physical needs can be entrusted to the good care of another person. Trust enables you to be your true self in your relationship with another person. Trust begins with your ability to trust the 'Me' in you. Intimacy allows you to connect the 'Me' in you with the 'Me' in another person.

Intimacy allows you to share the essence of who you are with another person. This special connection fulfills the natural need to belong.

Love is the ability to give unconditional affection, support, trust and intimacy to yourself, and then love others as you love yourself. You cannot give what you do not already have. This is why it's so important to learn to love the 'Me' in you. The love you have for you can easily be shared with others.

If the information you collect suggests that you terminate the dating relationship, this information should not be ignored. The purpose of dating is to collect additional information. Why would you collect information and not use it to make your decision? Albeit disappointing, you should welcome feedback that you did not hope to receive. For instance, if differences in religious beliefs, culture, or parenting styles become apparent and create an insurmountable chasm in the dating relationship, it is okay to compassionately end the relationship. This will save you time, money and heartache over the long run. The option of resuming the previous friendship stage can also be discussed. Again, your assessment of the quality and viability of the dating relationship is shaped by evidence-based information, not only by your emotional needs. If the information collected points to advancing the dating relationship, you can begin to discuss higher stage relationships such as marriage and companionship. You can expect success in these relationships because they will contain substance. The marriage or companionship will be able to sustain and withstand formidable challenges because it has character, quality, importance, and a strong constitution.

All relationships, at any stage, begin with your relationship with the 'Me' in you. Your relationship with the 'Me' in you is your North Star and is used to guide and manage all of your relationships. It is time to become re-acquainted with your 'Me'. Reconnecting with the 'Me' in you is a **process**, not an event. This process will require you to be patient with yourself. You will need a new commitment and renewed dedication to rekindle your relationship with you. The following post is an example of such commitment and dedication:

BEING MYSELF

I am the only 'me' I've got. I am unique. There are two major parts of me. There is the inside 'me' and the outside 'me'.

The outside me is what you see. The way I act, the image I portray, the way I look and the things I do. The outside me is very important. It is my messenger to the world and much of my outside me is what communicates with you. I value what I have done, the way I look and what I share with you. The inside 'me' knows all my feelings, my secret ideas, and my many hopes and dreams. Sometimes I let you know a little bit about the inside 'me' and sometimes it's a very private part of myself.

Even though there are an enormous number of people in this world, no one is exactly like 'me'. I take full responsibility for 'me' and the more I learn about myself the more responsibility I am going to take. You see, my 'me' is my responsibility. As I know myself more and more I find out that I am an OK person. I've done some good things in life because I am a good person. I have accomplished some things in my life because I am a competent person. I know some special people because I am worth knowing. I celebrate the many things I have done for myself.

I've also made some mistakes. I can learn from them. I have also known some people who did not appreciate me. I do not need to keep those people in my life. I've wasted some precious time. I can make new choices now. As long as I can see, hear, feel, think, change, grow and behave. I have great possibilities, and I am going to grow and love and be and celebrate. I am worth it!!!

by Wendi S. (posted 9/9/08)

Let's start by assessing where you are today in your relationship with your 'Me'. Complete the following 'Is My Relation**Ship** with Me Sinking' questionnaire. Rate yourself on each statement as it reflects your own relationship. Each statement indicates how you interact with the 'Me' in you. This is not pass or fail. There is no pressure to 'fake good' on this questionnaire. There is no need to feel ashamed about your score if it is low and you are not obligated to share your results with anyone but you. It is an honest conversation with the 'Me' in you. It is intended to point out areas wherein you can begin to improve your relationship with your 'Me'.

Is My RelationShip with Me Sinking Questionnaire

Please rate the following as it reflects your opinion of the 'Me' in you (1 is low and 5 is high)

1.	EFFECTIVE COMMUNICATION WITH 'ME'	1	2	3	4	5
2.	ABILITY TO LISTEN TO 'ME'	1	2	3	4	5
3.	TRUSTWORTHY TO 'ME'	1	2	3	4	5
4.	DEPENDABLE TO 'ME'	1	2	3	4	5
5.	ABILITY TO LOVE 'ME'	1	2	3	4	5
6.	ABILITY TO RECEIVE LOVE FROM 'ME'	1	2	3	4	5
7.	ABILITY TO BE INTIMATE WITH 'ME'	1	2	3	4	5
8.	ABILITY TO GUIDE 'ME'	1	2	3	4	5
9.	ABILITY TO MEET MY EXPECTATIONS OF 'ME'	1	2	3	4	5
10.	OVERALL SATISFACTION WITH MY RELATIONSHIP WITH 'ME'	1	2	3	4	5

Score________

50 points is maximum score.
A minimum score of 35 is required for healthy relationship.
A score of less than 35 points is a T1 relationShip.

Although it is not required, it is a good idea to share your findings with a healthy thinking person, a spiritual leader, or a behavioral health professional. At this point, do not trust yourself, alone, to evaluate your relationship with you. You may be too close to the forest to see the trees. If your results indicate you have a T1 relationship with your 'Me', the following 'Me' exercise can help improve your relationship:

Go to a local store that sells toys. Look for the shelf that contains lots of small (2 inches tall) cuddly animals such as teddy bears, lions or any animal you like. Pick one that resonates with you, purchase it and take it home. Give your little buddy a name that is meaningful to you. It can be any name you choose including your own. This represents the 'Me' in you. This is you when you were only 5 years old. You were innocent, loving, caring and eager to explore the world. The 'Me' in you has not and will never change. Your perception of your 'Me' changed, but your 'Me' can never change. You are still as worthwhile today as you were at 5 years old. Take your 'little you' everywhere you go. You may feel silly or awkward at first, but don't give up. It is small and will fit in your shirt pocket; purse; on the consul in your car; on your desk at work; and on your night table in your bedroom. You will be constantly reminded that you do, in fact, exist. You are a real person with your own unique ideas, thoughts and feelings. Talk to you throughout the day and particularly when you feel anxious, sad or lonely. Tell yourself that you care; you will not leave you; you can count on you; and that you have your full support. Most of all let you know that you do not have to be afraid because you are more able to protect you today. You are able to calm and soothe yourself without the aid of food; drugs; other negative behaviors; or T1 people who do not represent your best interest. Practice treating you as though you are your best friend. If you misplace yourself for a time, relocate your little best friend and continue to keep you by your side at all times. This exercise is designed to facilitate **self-reparation**. Eventually, this practice will help repair your relationship and bring you closer to the 'Me' in you.

It is common for you to initially feel uncomfortable being close to you as you practice your 'Me' exercise. Do not be dissuaded and practice this exercise daily or as much as possible. After a 90 day period of consistent practice, re-take the 'Is My Relation**Ship** with Me Sinking' questionnaire and observe any evidence of progress you are making as reflected by an increase, however slight, in your total score. Consult a healthy thinking person or a knowledgeable individual outside of your T1 social network regarding your findings. This exercise will be challenging because you may be easily distracted by focusing on things other than yourself. You will need to improve your ability to focus on you. Let's discuss what you will need to keep the focus on your 'Me'.

6

KEEP THE FOCUS ON ME

'KFOM'

Keep the Focus on Me (KFOM) is often used as a simple 'saying' or phrase by many people. You may have heard someone else use this phrase and then picked it up for yourself. You may say in conversation, 'I'm just trying to keep the focus on me'. In other words, you are simply telling yourself things like don't respond; just be quiet; or it's time to be alone and away from others. So you may sleep in another bedroom or in the basement for a few days; then go back to the negative situation, time and time again. Until now, KFOM has only meant that you were taking a temporary time-out. You do not know the real meaning of KFOM because you have not practiced KFOM since you were a child.

KFOM means to take full and consistent responsibility for your spiritual, mental, and emotional wellbeing. KFOM reflects your insistence upon self-care and self-responsibility. KFOM is defined as you being the center of activity, attraction, or attention. Keeping the activity, attraction and attention on you is a full-time job. If you begin to take days off, you can become complacent. Overtime, KFOM becomes a personal obligation and a new way of life. It is a constant process of 'doing for you'. If you are not doing for you, you are undoing. It is always one or the other. You cannot live in personal freedom while in neutral. As soon as you start to feel down, know that you have stopped doing for you and you have taken the focus off you. Any sign of T1 Thinking is always a signal or warning that you have taken the focus off you.

KFOM is a conscious, deliberate recognition, and respect for the need to give to your Self over and above a need to give to others. KFOM is not egocentrism. Egocentrics live in their own world and cannot accept that reality may be different from their perception. It is important to note that KFOM is not a form of T1 Thinking. In T1 Thinking, your need to give to others is an un-avowed '**quid pro quo**' because it is how you get:

» approval

» self-esteem

» value

» your reason for being

» your sense of being in control

» your sense of security

» to avoid rejection and abandonment; and

» to believe that 'someone' cares about you.

You have given to others before giving to yourself because you have been **afraid** not to give. Your giving has been designed to prevent a feeling of utter loss and devastation. This process has not and will not work. It's time to change.

KFOM is a recognition and commitment to nurture you. T1 Thinking causes you to falsely believe that this process is already completed. It is not completed. Continue learning to nurture yourself and nurturing others will follow.

There are several principles you will have to learn in order to KFOM. You are encouraged to **study** and **practice** these principles often.

PRINCIPLES OF KFOM

1. **Admit** to your own existence: Say, 'I am somebody'. 'I do exist'. 'I am who the Creator says I am'. You cannot allow your job, your synagogue, church or mosque, your mate, sick relatives, or **you** to stop you from KFOM. To admit to your own existence is not a simple affirmation. An affirmation is restating a current belief to be fact or to be true. i.e., self confidence; intelligence or loveable. **You cannot affirm what you do not currently believe**. To admit to your own existence is a confession. You acknowledge your existence to be true. To admit also implies a previous reluctance to disclose the truth about your existence. So, admitting to your existence was preceded by denial of your own existence.

While in denial, you refuse to accept, believe, recognize, or acknowledge your existence. Furthermore, you have acted to refute your own existence by trying to prove it to be wrong, false or incorrect. These actions are apparent when you allow yourself to be mistreated and disrespected by others (and vice-versa). Your attempt to refute your existence is evident when you allow others to redefine you as they see you. You may also tell yourself that you are not good enough to exist.

In order to admit to your own existence, you must be willing to feel **uncomfortable**. It takes time to feel comfortable with your own Self, especially when you have denied its existence for so many years. Expect and allow yourself to feel uncomfortable for awhile. Feeling uncomfortable will not harm you and this feeling will eventually become less noticeable.

You may also feel empty because you don't know how it feels to exist. You may feel like 'nothing' because you are not accustomed to feeling your own existence.

You may feel insecure and vulnerable while learning to admit to your own existence. This is ok. Just remember this is a new experience and you will begin to feel less insecure and less vulnerable over time.

You may also feel alone while learning to admit to your own existence. You and T1 others are not sure how to relate to you. You may be unsure of what to do or say. Detaching from T1 people can make you feel alone; but stay on your new course. Challenge these uncomfortable, phobic feelings head-on.

2. Concentrate on you and guard against distractions and distracters. This means that you should not entertain or take on other people's problems and negativity. This is drama and there is no healthy benefit in your participation in drama. If you reduce your participation in drama by 80%, you will simultaneously have an 80% increase in available time to KFOM. You can no longer afford to devote 80% of your time being comfortable and complacent while participating in drama.

3. Recognize that you share the responsibility for what T1 people do to you as long as you are connected to them. As an adult, you have placed and kept yourself in T1 situations. Imagine sticking your finger in an electrical outlet, and then complaining that you were jolted by electricity. It would not make sense to call and report your behavior to the electric company. You would be told that you cannot knowingly stick your finger in an electrical outlet, get electrocuted, and then complain when electricity does what it

is known to do. It is time to stop blaming T1 Thinking people for being who they think they are and for doing the things they are known to do. It is time to focus on changing your own T1 Thinking. Changing your own thinking will have a positive effect on everyone around you, whether they like it or not. Expect T1 people not to like your healthy change. They will not recognize the 'new' you. You should also expect that someone will recognize the new 'light' in you and begin to ask you to help them change their thinking. This person may be a relative or a person that has observed you from a distance. There will be opportunities to share your experiences with others who are searching for themselves.

4. KFOM is a unilateral, not a joint, decision to hold yourself fully **accountable** for your own happiness and wellbeing. It has nothing to do with your T1 mate, T1 family members or T1 associates. You are liable, answerable, and responsible for creating and maintaining your own state of happiness and wellbeing. You are fully accountable for what you do to and for you. Those around you who are unhappy cannot help you. Anyone, regardless of their title or the title you give them, who has T1 Thinking cannot help you to have healthy thinking. Healthy thinkers look at life in a balanced way; not

through rose-colored or pessimistic glasses. Healthy thinking requires you to hold yourself accountable for your thoughts. You are accountable for identifying, challenging and changing any idea that does not represent your best interest.

5. Pay close **attention** to your thoughts/feelings and correct them when necessary. T1 Thinking can become a 'norm' for you over the years and can cause you not to pay attention to your thinking. For instance, in T1 relationships, it is common for parents not to get along with each other; it is routine to witness physical or emotional abuse while growing up; it is typical to think that it's ok to beat yourself up; it is acceptable to get emotionally involved with people you do not know and who do not know themselves; and it is almost traditional to have multiple failed 'marriages' and failed relationships. For example, meeting a person with four failed relationships brings up no red flags for T1 persons. They convince themselves that a relationship that was 'dead on arrival' will suddenly spring to life in the near future.

   It has also become norm for you not to know you, not to trust you, and not to trust your Creator.

You can change this tendency by beginning to pay attention to thoughts that represent your best interest. Practice paying attention to at least 2 healthy thoughts for every 1 negative thought. Close your eyes and ask yourself for permission to create a healthier environment in your mind. There is no state or federal law that says you are required to continue to entertain disparaging ideas. Paying close attention to your thoughts can and must be done, even within an adverse family environment

6. Practice healthy self-engagement and healthy self-talk. It is important that you recognize that you have not spent enough time at healthy engagement with your Self. If you do not accept this fact, then you will not see the need to change it. If you desire personal freedom, the evidence will include your willingness to devote meaningful time practicing healthy self-engagement. You can do this in several ways:

   a) Speaking with someone who has healthy thinking. You cannot practice healthy self-engagement by talking to those who are not healthy. Begin speaking with a behavioral health professional, a spiritual leader or another knowledgeable, emotionally competent person. Engaging others who are healthy will help you learn healthy self-engagement.

b) Speak to yourself. When you are upset, practice calming and soothing your Self. Remind your Self that you do not have to panic. Take a moment to just breathe. You can also join Yoga and meditation classes to facilitate healthy self-engagement.

c) Practice staying in today and not racing into next week or next month. Try to live just for today or in some cases, just for the next hour.

d) Tell your 'Me' that he/she is safe with you today. Your 'Me' still becomes afraid sometimes but you are more than able to protect your Self today.

e) Ask your Self, 'how are you doing'? 'Do you need anything from me'? Then be responsive to your Self.

f) Stop being critical of your Self. You can tell yourself to stop the criticism and it will stop. You have to be consistent with this demand.

g) Stop needing to be perfect until you find at least one human being who is perfect.

h) Stop giving in to phobias and start challenging them. Phobia is not real.

The following KFOM daily checklist is another tool that will help you practice and learn how to KFOM. It will help restore your relationship with the 'Me' in you.

KEEP THE FOCUS ON ME DAILY CHECKLIST

The following is a list of daily activities that will assist me in keeping my attention on me. I will refer to this list several times daily until I am able to focus on me and consistently do what represents my best interest.

- o Admit to my own existence; I Am Who my Creator Says I Am.
- o Protect myself from my own negative distractions and other negative distractions.
- o Stop blaming T1people for being T1 and continue working to reduce my own T1 Thinking.
- o I am fully accountable for my happiness and wellbeing. I realize that those who are unhappy and unhealthy cannot help me.
- o Pay close attention to my thoughts and correct them as needed.
- o Practice healthy self engagement and healthy self-talk.
- o Practice until I achieve 70% thinking. When I am less than 70%, I will work to promptly return to 70% thinking.

- I will learn something new about who the Creator says I am daily.

- I will increase my interaction with healthy individuals outside my 'comfortable' and familiar T1 network.

- I will ensure (daily) that I manage my thinking and I will not allow my thinking to manage me.

7

FORGIVENESS IN T1 RELATIONSHIPS

A lack of forgiveness can be a barrier to a healthy relationship with the 'Me' in you and limit your ability to KFOM. **Forgiveness** in healthy relationships involves the use of free will to release resentments, negative attitudes and negative feelings toward another who has committed an offense against you. There is good reason to feel hurt, disrespected, harmed, or violated. The evidence against the offender is compelling and clearly violates your sense of trust, safety, security, and/or devotion. The person who committed the offense must be **competent**, but failed in his/her responsibility. Nevertheless, in the face of overwhelming evidence that a transgression was committed, you voluntarily release any and all feelings of ill-will, anger, ideas of retaliation, or any desire to 'get even' with the offender. Forgiveness is one of the greatest gifts you can give to yourself. Forgiveness also protects your mental and emotional wellbeing.

Forgiveness takes on a different meaning in T1 relationships. You can develop unfounded resentments towards others. Few, if any, of your current resentments are brand new. Your resentments are life-long and began when you were a child. Children do not have enough life experience or maturity to accurately interpret the behaviors of T1 adults. Children who grow up in T1 families are challenged to make accurate perceptions of the family chaos they see and experience. For instance, children who grow up in T1families may observe parental arguments and fighting. They are likely entangled in the web of parental separation and divorce. They become frightened and insecure when parents are emotionally unavailable. Children become confused by parental substance abuse. They begin to suffer through parental condemnation and verbal abuse. Children also learn how to care for their parents and they grow up before their time. These children are referred to as **parentified** children.

It is extremely difficult for a child to develop an accurate perception or interpretation of their experiences while under the care of T1 adults. A child's perception and interpretation of T1 behaviors in T1 families will be false. Children draw false conclusions about T1 adults as a way of trying to make sense of T1 behaviors. These false conclusions become resentments by the time they reach adulthood. For example as a child, you conclude that people important to you will not respect you; they cannot be trusted; and they will not love you. You resent dad for not being a father to you. You resent your parents for never saying or showing that they loved you. The food, clothing and shelter were great, but you resent your parents for never saying they are proud of you. You resent your sister for believing she could do nothing wrong, while in her eyes, you could do nothing right. You invariably get stuck in these and other unfounded resentments for years.

These conclusions are false because the offenses were committed by T1 adults who were not competent in the areas of their transgression. As an adult, you resent T1 individuals important to you for 'not being there' for you; for not showing love and appreciation for you; for not applauding your strengths and successes; and for 'making' you feel inferior. You don't realize that your unfounded resentments towards individuals, with whom you currently share T1 relationships, are based on the false conclusions of a 5 year old child who did the best he or she could to make sense out of T1 adult non-sense. Your current unfounded resentments have a basis in fact, but not in truth.

FACT VS. TRUTH

Mark Twain said, **"It ain't what you don't know that gets you in trouble. It's what you know for sure that just ain't so".** What you know is a fact. A **fact** is an actual event that occurs within reality, but facts alone may not be reality. They are events that occur within reality. Now, the **truth** is the most **accurate interpretation** of those facts. The truth reflects the actual state of reality and conforms to reality.

Trouble begins where there is a lack of understanding of the difference between facts and truth. When what you know for sure just ain't so, people who are not guilty are convicted of crimes and spend time in prison. When what you know for sure just ain't so, bias and stigma are promulgated against people because of their culture, religion, age, dis-**Abilities**, gender, or sexual preference. Likewise, resentment in T1 relationships is driven by what you know for sure that just ain't so. To illustrate, you may harbor resentment towards your father for several facts. He was not 'there' for you. He did not keep his promises to you. He did not say or show that he loved you. Yet, he married his third wife and lived in her home with her children. You have asked yourself a thousand times, 'why did he not do that for me'? It would be naïve to think that your father would be any different while living with his third wife and her children. The truth is that your father never learned to 'be there' for anyone. His father was not 'there' for him. Your father was raised on broken promises by his father. He simply treated you the same way. Your father never learned to show love because love was not shown to him. The most accurate interpretation of the facts is that your father unknowingly suffers with T1 Thinking; he is enmeshed in T1 relationships; and he did the best he could do with what he had. If your father was capable of being the father you deserved, he would have been that father. That's the truth. Your resentments are unfounded and based on facts. You have every right to feel disappointed and sad for not having a father; but as an adult, you have a responsibility to let go of your false conclusions (developed at age 5) about your father and embrace the truth. This responsibility holds for any T1 Thinking person that disappointed you. You will eventually exchange your unfounded resentment with empathy for them. You will also be able to see them for who they think they are, rather than who you need them to be for you.

This distinction of fact vs. truth suggests that forgiveness may not be applicable in T1 relationships. Since offenses committed in T1 relationships are based on facts, they may not reflect reality. Some facts in T1families and relationships are hard to ignore. Nevertheless, offenses committed in T1 relationships are **surreal**, which is a mixture of facts and fantasy. You cannot forgive someone for not doing what they were never capable of doing for you. For instance, forgiveness does not apply when you resent a person who always walked around with a set of carpentry tools, but failed miserably at remodeling your kitchen. The person was not a competent carpenter. If the person was widely known to be a competent carpenter and he failed miserably at remodeling your kitchen, you would have a basis for resentment. You could also forgive this person because he/she had the skills necessary to do the job; but the person failed to do so. Remember, while you have a right to your feelings, forgiveness does not apply when your resentments are unfounded.

This perspective of forgiveness also applies to your relationship with the 'ME' in you. As a result of your own T1 Thinking, you have developed misperceptions about the 'Me' in you. You have discounted yourself; you have disliked yourself; you have said that you are not good enough, despite your many successes; you have disapproved of yourself; and you have decided that you are not worthy of loving the 'Me' in you. Many of the behaviors you committed to justify these feelings towards yourself happened after you were 5 years old and continued into adulthood. You may have subsequently abused drugs/alcohol, began abusing food, associated with people who did not represent your best interest, dropped out of school, lost jobs, lost relationships, and/or experienced other self-imposed disappointments. Now, try to think of one offense that was committed against you by your 5 year old Self. You can take as long as you would like to identify an offense and you will come up empty. **The truth is that the 'ME' in you has never committed a wrongful act against you.** Yet, you have punished your 'ME' as though every indiscretion was caught on tape. There are no offenses and there is no tape. Although it is not required, you can apologize to the 'ME' in you and ask for forgiveness. The 'ME' in you has already forgiven you; does not hold resentments against you; and loves you as much as ever, despite what you have put your Self through. This may be hard for you to believe, but it is the truth. Spend as much time as you need to internalize this revelation. Simply reading is not enough. Think about the truth that the 'ME' in you has never committed an offense against you; journal about it often; and speak with healthy individuals (outside of your T1network) or a behavioral health professional about it for more clarity and understanding.

You can also utilize the 'empty chair' technique wherein you place an empty chair within a comfortable distance from you. Imagine the 'ME' in you sitting in the chair. Begin speaking with you; let you know how you feel about you; apologize to you and ask you for forgiveness for mistakenly mistreating you, knowing that you are already forgiven. This exercise can be challenging, but stick with it. Start practicing even if you don't know what to say. Just 'be' with you. Begin with a 5 minute conversation several days per week and expand as you are able. The more you practice, the easier it will become and you will begin to place the empty chair closer and closer to you. Eventually, you will only need one chair for you because you are beginning to let go of your resentments and the negative, surreal experiences of the past.

8

LET IT GO

In order to live, thrive, and prosper in personal freedom, you must learn to let go of the past. It is time to tear down the imaginary walls of the past that prevent you from enjoying the blessings of today and the promises of tomorrow. Except for drama, none of your troubles happened today. Your troubles happened many years ago; but you feel as though they happened this morning. The time has come, and it is ok for you to let go of:

» guilt, which is based on facts, not truth;

» shame, which is based on facts, not truth;

» resentment, which is based on facts, not truth;

» anger, which is based on facts, not truth;

» low self-worth; which is based on facts, not truth;

- » feelings of not fitting in, which are based on facts, not truth;
- » feelings of not being good enough, which are based on facts, not truth;
- » feelings of insecurity, which are based on facts, not truth;
- » false beliefs, which are based on facts, not truth; and
- » self loathing, which is based on facts, not truth.

If you decide to stay in these dark places that represent your past, there is no healthy reprieve. There is no healthy resolution. Some of the T1 people connected to these dark places are deceased. Those still alive have not changed or may not want to change. In some instances, holding onto the past allows you to stay close to familiar pain. You do not deserve to live in pain and it is ok to begin to let go of your familiar emotional pain.

It is ok to take time to grieve your past. You have a right to feel sorrow about your past, especially your childhood. Childhood is a special moment that comes once in a lifetime. It is a time of innocence for all children; it is a time to be care free; it is a time to explore and ask questions; it is a time to learn **who you are**; and a time to begin to develop the tools needed to grow-up to be a happy, productive adult. A child's interaction with healthy parents and a healthy family is **vital** during this special time. Vital means to live. Vital is something that is necessary for the maintenance of life. Children who do not experience healthy interactions with their parents and family are deprived of vital interactions. It is vital that children receive and learn genuine love; genuine trust; genuine intimacy; and positive self-esteem. These vitals are central to the maintenance of life and the achievement of personal freedom. It is ok to grieve the past where it involves the loss of this vital period of your life, your childhood. You should talk about your loss; share about your loss; journal about your loss; and pray about your loss.

Other than the loss of your childhood, holding on to other grim parts of your past must be released. Begin to release your past by recognizing it as a **surreal** experience. T1 surrealism is an experience marked by the intense reality of a nightmare. Surreal experiences include witnessing irrational, disjointed, bizarre and nonsensical events. These statements are examples of T1 surrealism:

'Dad loved his 2nd and 3rd wives and their 6 children, but he didn't love us'.

'I was certain that my 4th marriage would be successful, but it wasn't'.

'I accepted my mom's drinking, but I cannot accept that she didn't love me'.

'My partner and I communicated well after we met; during her relapse; and after I picked her up from the detox; but after dating 6 months and getting married, things fell apart'

'My dad traveled all over the country taking care of his successful company. My mom worked tirelessly as a doctor while taking care of her patients. I had the house all to myself since I was eight. Now I am 21 years old, with no life; I don't know what went wrong or why I let them down'.

Much of the past you hold on to is associated with T1 family members and their illogical behavior toward you as a child. It is surreal because what you have believed to be true was not real. It looked and felt real; but it was actually surreal. Your adult caretakers would have to be healthy in order for your past experiences to be real. It is difficult to distinguish real from surreal just like it is difficult to distinguish fear from phobia. Fear and reality are the same experiences. Phobia and surreal are the same experiences. It is surreal to think you are in an intimate relationship that is not intimate. It is surreal for you to think that you are in a trusting relationship with a person who is not trustworthy. It is surreal to think that an alcoholic parent refused to love you. It is surreal for you to think that you are not good enough for any partner because you could not maintain your relationship with your ex-partner, who could not maintain a relationship with four ex-partners prior to you. Remember that two broken pieces, when put together, do not make one whole; they make two broken pieces put together.

You do not have to continue to talk about your past as though it was a real experience. Your past is surreal because T1 relationships are surreal. You cannot place unrealistic expectations on people with T1 Thinking and expect to receive a response that is based in reality. T1 Thinking persons who do not love themselves cannot be blamed for not loving you.

Begin to let go of your surreal experiences. Let it go and begin to discuss your past as a new story that is based in reality and truth. Give a true explanation of the events and incidents in your life. A true account of your life reflects your:

» resilience

» strength

» courage

Your true story says:

✓ 'I'm still here in spite of what I went through';

✓ 'I'm supposed to be here because I belong';

✓ 'I belong just like everyone else';

✓ 'I do fit in';

✓ 'I'm a survivor'; and

✓ 'I'm strong'.

Tell a story that truly validates you, your life and you as a child of your Creator. Tell a story of hope, self confidence, enjoyment, and optimism so that others may be inspired to embark on a journey to personal freedom.

Hope is not a fantasy. Hope is not a passive exercise. Hope is a real expectation to live with happiness, joy and peace of mind. Hope is a **real** belief, with a high sense of certainty, that your expectation will come true.

Self confidence involves learning to trust the 'Me' in you again. Begin to free your Self from uncertainty and shame. You can begin to have confidence in your Self without being conceited or arrogant.

You can begin to give your Self permission to experience enjoyment in life. You don't have to be afraid of joy and contentment as though these feelings represent a bad omen. Enjoyment is a natural reward of living in personal freedom.

You can set aside your pessimistic view of yourself for optimism. Optimism allows you to pursue personal freedom with eager anticipation of the best that life has to offer you. Therefore, hope; self confidence; enjoyment; and optimism serve as the mental framework for your pursuit of personal freedom. This mental framework is important in order to achieve personal freedom.

9

IMPORTANT

Your effort to restore a healthy relationship with the 'Me' in you requires significant effort. Your willingness to provide significant effort depends on the level of **importance** you place upon your Self. If you feel that you are unimportant; you will provide little effort. Like most other people, your best effort is placed on work that is important to you, regardless of whether it is good, bad or indifferent. If excessive eating is deemed important to you, you will devote all the effort necessary to eat. If a particular relationship with a person is important to you, you will exhaust every available opportunity you have to maintain that relationship, good or bad. You are driven by what is important to you. Likewise, you are less involved with matters that are not important to you. This has major implications for the task at hand. Ask yourself, 'how important have I been to myself'? On a scale of 1 to 10, rate the average level of importance you have placed upon yourself over the course of your life to the present time. If you come up with a number of 7 or higher, you must have ample evidence to support this figure and you should review your findings and supporting evidence with a healthy person who is not part of your T1 network or with a behavioral health professional. If you have a history of T1 Thinking, that number is more likely to be an average of 5 or less. This means there is a 50% chance that you may be willing to devote the necessary time, energy and effort at restoring your relationship with the 'Me' in you. This suggests you are worth little more than a flip of a coin. Let's look at some changes you can begin to make to increase your level of importance.

You have devoted weeks, months and years of time and energy trying to be who other people wanted you to be; trying to make other people happy; and trying to keep other people in your life. Ask yourself, 'what do I have to show that my investment of time and energy was worth it'? You are far beyond the point of diminishing returns. While you were investing weeks, months and years of time and energy into others, who was investing in you? No one was investing in you spiritually, emotionally or otherwise.

Now is the time for you to shift your focus from those external people to your internal 'Me'. 'Important' is something indicative of significant worth. 'Important' is something of value in relationship. Say these words to yourself aloud: 'I have significant worth'. 'My relationship with 'Me' is valuable'. This is not a suggestion for you to become ego-centric. It is a reminder that you and your own needs are important. Let's take a look at how you get in your way of focusing on your own importance.

The 2nd Self vs. 'Me'

There is a part of you that is determined not to allow you to consider your Self first. There is a part of you that will not allow your 'Me' to be important to you. This is called your 2nd self. Your 2nd self is real and it is the embodiment of misinformation you received from T1 adults who were important to you as a child. Your thinking changed significantly when your 2nd self arrived on the scene, soon after your 5th birthday. As a child, you unconsciously realized that you would not be able to survive in face of the distress and insanity you were beginning to witness. Now enters your 2nd self, or alter-ego, which becomes adept at T1 Thinking, T1 perception, and T1 mal-adaptations to a T1family and environment. The original purpose of your 2nd self was to ensure your survival. For instance, your 2nd self learned that opiates numb emotional pain caused by sexual abuse and other trauma. Your 2nd self experimented with street drugs until it discovered that cocaine can give temporary relief from depression. Your 2nd self discovered that if you can keep secrets, people important to you will not leave you. They will 'like' you because you did not tell anyone what they did to you. Your 2nd self awakes you in the middle of the night so that you can eat again and feel less anxious. Your 2nd self scolds you and says that if you can learn how to keep the house super-clean, your partner will start loving you and will not verbally abuse you. Your 2nd self is not concerned about your importance, value or self-worth; it is only concerned about your survival in insane places. Your 5 year old 'Me' was not created for T1 relationships and related experiences.

Even though you have survived, your 2nd self does not want to relinquish its control over you. Moreover, your 2nd self is so determined to maintain control and direct your life that it is willing to attempt to destroy you. This is how you found yourself in unthinkable, life-threatening situations in your past. Your 2nd self, not T1 people important to you, is your arch enemy. Your greatest battle is between your 'Me' and 2nd self. The self you believe the most; the self in which you invest the most; the self you support the most; the self that is most **important** to you will win. **The 'Me' that conquers it's 2nd self, conquers all**. You will not face a greater challenge in life. Overcoming your T1 Thinking will defeat your 2nd self and restore your healthy self. You are able to win the battles of the 'selves'.

'Me' and Spirituality

The reason you are able to be triumphant in conquering your 2nd self is because your 'Me' is the spiritual embodiment of the Creator in you. Your 2nd self will give you all you can handle, but your 2nd self is no match for your Creator. The Creator is the author of all things, including you. Your Creator is the spiritual deity responsible for your existence. The Creator's spirit in you is the primary source of your value and importance. No person in your life has the power or authority to give or take away the importance your Creator placed within you. Your Creator's spirit in you is the essence of your 'Me'. The Creator's spirit and your 'Me' are one and the same. Without your Creator's spirit, you would not exist and you would not have intrinsic value. Your intrinsic value makes you important. It makes you important whether you know it or not; agree with it or not; accept it or not. No matter whom you mistakenly thought you were; no matter what you may have done; your Creator continues to abide in you and you remain important because of the Creator's spirit in you. Your Creator loves and values you and '**there is nothing you can do about it**'.

It is not the value of your home, cars, clothing, your corporation, bank account or any other material thing that gives you intrinsic value. Before you were born, your intrinsic value was freely given to you by your Creator. When you die and the spirit of your Creator leaves your body, your intrinsic value is lost. What is left of you is called remains. Your remains have no value. This is why a person's remains are promptly buried, burned, or borrowed by a medical institution for teaching and research. Because your Creator's spirit is the essence of who you are, you were born with certain traits of your Creator such as love, humility, faith, honesty, integrity, patience, gentleness and forgiveness. These traits represent the substance of your 'Me' or your true self. These were your original characteristics at birth and you continue to possess these characteristics as long as the Creator's spirit dwells within you. So don't give up on yourself and falsely believe that you are not salvageable. With guidance from those who have spiritual knowledge, you have every reason to be hopeful that you can reunite and rebuild your relationship with the Creator's spirit in you. The Creator's relationship with you is unchanged; you need to re-establish your relationship with the Creator.

Restoring your relationship with the 'Me' in you is a spiritual, not a religious, process. Restoring your relationship with the 'Me' in you is the same as restoring your relationship with your Creator. The more you learn about your Creator, the more you understand your Self.

It is not uncommon for T1 adults to give children a misleading or inadequate account of the spiritual basis for their existence. In the absence of a firm spiritual foundation beginning at an early age, you begin to view T1 adults important to you as '**gods**'. They have power and authority over you; they make judgments about you; they punish you; you make every effort to serve and please them; and you spend your life trying to get them to love you. You begin to pseudo-worship these individuals over the course of your life. You punish yourself time and time again for your inability to please these 'gods' and your inability to get them to love you. In effect, these T1 adults who are important to you subtly replace your Creator and become your gods. As an adult, you dedicate an overwhelming and unwarranted amount of time to these 'gods'. You refer to them as your mom, dad, grand-parent; children; partner; spouse; or 'friend'. You devote your life to them and that devotion has almost destroyed you. In practice, your 'god' is the person(s) you think about the most; attempt to please the most; give most of your time, money, and energy to; talk about the most; and/or cry about the most. If this person(s) is anyone other than the Creator, you are spiritually misled.

You can see how easy it is to develop an unfounded resentment towards your Creator. Your 'gods' let you down and your Creator gets the blame. Your resentment towards your Creator is unfounded because it is impossible for your Creator to let you down; to never care about you; or to withdraw love away from you. Your Creator has a permissive will that allows you to use your own will to serve the 'gods' you create for yourself. Serving your self-made 'gods' invariably leads to train wrecks. Your Creator has no desire for you to be in train wrecks; but your Creator can and has rescued you from many of your train wrecks. You will have to choose who you will believe and trust; your self-made 'gods' or your Creator. Your Creator loves you no matter which choice you make. Just know that you can only be important by believing and trusting who created you; that is your Creator.

Despite all that you have been through, you can still be the best you can be because of your Creator. You can begin to live your life to show your Creator how grateful you are for the spirit that is within you and the spirit that makes you important. You can live and work each day and say to your Creator, 'look at what I have done with the spirit you gave me'. You can use your spirit to build, teach, lead, volunteer or for any constructive endeavor. You can express your gratitude in your own unique way. Strive each day to say 'thank you Creator' for sharing your spirit with 'Me'. Ask yourself, 'What can I do today to say thank you Creator'? This is a question of a person who is **important**.

MY WILL

The Creator has endowed you with a **Will.** Although the Creator's spirit in you makes you important, your importance can be stymied by your **Will**. Your Will is the **power** or **control** over your own actions and/or emotions. Your Will gives you the power and authority to exercise **choice** or **self-determination**. Although the Creator views you as important, you can exercise your power and authority to deny your intrinsic importance. While you may point an accusatory finger at others, it is by your own power and authority that you can be:

- unhappy
- distrustful

- fearful
- anxious
- fake
- angry
- afraid of intimacy

By your own power and authority, you can also place the needs of others ahead of your own; continue to reinjure yourself emotionally; and live beneath your privilege.

It is by your own power and authority (Will) that you can say 'I am not going to allow myself to be important'. When you do everything, within your power and authority, to express your importance within a T1 relationship, this is a clear statement of your Will not to be important. This represents negative Will and it causes you to live your life in contradiction. You say that you want what is best for you, but the evidence suggest that you want the worse for you. For instance, you say you love your family, but the evidence shows that you can't get along with your family. You say that you want to be happily married, but the evidence shows that you're miserable. You say that you want to be in good physical health, but the evidence shows that you don't get proper exercise, get proper rest, or follow a healthy diet. In order for you to receive what you deserve out of life, your Will for your life must be consistent with the Creator's Will for your life. Here is where mistakes are often made. When you encounter a major problem, you ask the Creator for a solution;

then you implement your own solution; and you get angry at the Creator for the poor results. You pray to the Creator for a partner. Within a matter of days, you find a partner on your own. When the 'wheels fall off' of the relationship, you blame the Creator for all the drama and for your disappointment. The Creator gave you a Will and permits you to implement your own Will. When your life is in shambles, you have to stop and ask yourself, 'Whose Will am I following?' When you feel that you are not where you should be in life, you are exercising your own will. When you remain stuck in T1 relationships, you are exercising your own will. When you consistently do the things that do not represent your best interest, you are exercising your own will. When you allow your T1 relationships to adversely impact your children, you are exercising your own will.

How satisfied are you with your results? If you are not satisfied, your Will and your Creator's Will for you must become alike. Spiritual distrust can increase your reliance on your own Will, and prevent you from increasing your reliance on the Creator's Will for your life. Let's start to improve from where you are now with a self-assessment of your Will and your Importance.

Self-Assessment
My Will and My Importance

I will indicate my agreement with the following statements by placing my initials in the space provided. I will only initial those statements with which I agree or that I am willing to change **now**. I can initial other statements in the future as I become willing to increase my importance in those areas. I will not initial a statement that does not honestly reflect my present belief and will. I must show evidence to support the accuracy of each statement that I initial.

1. I believe it is the Creator's Will for me to be Important. _____

2. It is my Will for me to be Important. _____

3. It is my Will to treat me as though I am Important in all situations. _____

4. It is my Will and Important to me to develop healthy thinking. _____

5. It is my Will and Important to me to learn how to stop depending on emotionally needy people. _____

6. It is my Will and Important to me to stop criticizing Me. _____

7. It is my Will and Important to me to stop scaring myself with phobia. _____

8. It is my Will and Important to me to forgive myself. _____

9. It is my Will and Important to me to identify my spiritual and emotional weaknesses and seek help to strengthen these areas. _____

10. It is my Will and Important to me to make the most important change in the world, Me. _____

You should take as much time as you need to apply your initials to any statement on your self-assessment. You can take weeks or even months if necessary. You should not complete your self-assessment in five minutes or less. You are important enough to take as much time as you need to honestly assess where you stand today. There is no pass or fail. This is an honest conversation with you and about your willingness to be as important as your Creator says you are. Just begin to **know** this conversation must take place if you are to realize your intrinsic importance. Your willingness to be important to your Self will help you overcome years of self-devaluation experienced at the hands of other T1 individuals and by your 2nd self. Your importance is not external. Your importance is imbedded in the spirit given to you by your Creator, which is the center of who you are. You should review your self-assessment regularly and do not be afraid to ask for help when needed. It is a good idea to get an objective opinion from someone who is knowledgeable and not part of your T1 network.

Remind yourself of your importance every day despite the misinformation you will continue to receive from your T1 network and your 2nd self. When you are able to honestly initial at least 7 out of 10 items on your self-assessment, your level of importance will show significant improvement; your social landscape will begin to change and reflect a reduced number of T1 relationships; you will slowly increase members of your new healthy social network; and your healthier relationship with your Self will speed up your journey to personal freedom.

10

THE BASICS OF PERSONAL FREEDOM

You deserve to live in personal freedom. Say this out loud, 'I deserve my personal freedom'. It is important that you say this with strong belief and conviction because it is true. Personal freedom requires skill at taking good care of you. This has been an alien idea and you may have never been taught to take good care of your Self. There is far more to taking good care of your Self than good hygiene, a good haircut, or getting a manicure. Self-care is basic to personal freedom. It is time for you to practice self-care and you are encouraged to demand this change of yourself. You may not have been challenged to take care of your Self until now. You have always been able to 'get-by', but that will not work any-more. There are seven **basic** tools you will need to live in personal freedom and they are as follows:

1. **Personal Responsibility**: It is your job to take care of you. It is your job to make sure that you are ok. No one else is responsible for making

you better or happy. You must actively accept personal responsibility for you. You are your keeper. You cannot be your brother or sister's keeper until you learn how to keep you.

It is your job to make sure that you are ok spiritually. If you self-examine and find that you are not spiritually healthy, it is your responsibility to take yourself to a mountain top; the seashore; a synagogue, church, mosque; or wherever you can get your spiritual needs met.

It is your responsibility to make sure you are ok emotionally. If you find that you cannot focus, concentrate, sleep well, or have trouble remembering things, it is your job to seek help to ensure your emotional wellbeing. If you don't take care of you emotionally, who will take care of you? It is unacceptable for you to be irresponsible and not take good care of you. You must come face to face with this reality today. You have to answer for your own conduct. You can no longer rob, cheat and steal from you by not holding you responsible for your emotional wellbeing.

You are responsible for seeking what represents your best interest. When you make decisions, you are responsible for ensuring they consistently represent your best interest. You can no longer stand idle while your best interests go unrepresented by you. Now is the time for you to take responsibility for you.

2. **Personal Accountability**: Accountability works well with responsibility. If you find yourself behaving in an irresponsible manner, it is your job to hold yourself accountable for your behavior. If you do not handle a situation well, it's no longer simply another bad job. You must hold you accountable when you don't do what's in your best interest spiritually, mentally, emotionally and when you don't behave appropriately. You have to provide you with a reasonable explanation for what you do in all four areas. This is not an excuse, but an acceptable explanation. If you know you are downtrodden mentally or emotionally, you cannot allow this to go on day after day, or week after week. You can identify a solution that will help you repair this part of your being. You can speak with another healthy person; seek counseling with a behavioral health specialist; you can meditate; or take other concrete steps to help resolve your difficulty. When you exercise good responsibility, you can hold yourself accountable by saying to you that you did a really good job and that you handled the situation very well. Kudos is ok.

3. **Self Discipline**: This tool requires you to exercise restraint over your spontaneous thoughts and emotions. You can buy things

you can't afford before you know it; eat certain unhealthy foods and not realize how much you have been eating until several days later; or experience harmful feelings and run with them for several weeks. As you exercise restraint over these areas, you can enjoy a better relationship with you. Learning to exercise self discipline will help you enjoy better relationships with others while you live in personal freedom. You have to apply constructive discipline to yourself when you do things that do not represent your best interest. A simple review and discussion of what went wrong and how you can prevent it should suffice. Mistakes will happen because personal freedom is not about perfection; it's about learning to be human.

4. **Stewardship**: This tool represents your responsibility to actively direct your own affairs of life with skill and with care. It is your job to manage or supervise you. You have to step aside and watch what you do spiritually, mentally, emotionally and behaviorally. You oversee all of your activities. A good supervisor provides redirection when things go awry and helps put things back on course. It is your job to watch over you. No one else should have to call attention to your behavior. When they do, you get upset at them. You should point it out to yourself and take action to correct it.

It is your job to manage your affairs as though you are a maestro standing in front of an orchestra directing ego-syntonic music. This represents behavior that is consistent with your Self. If you begin to play ego-dystonic musical notes, which represents behavior that is distressing to your Self, correct them. Ego-dystonic notes create noise in your life. If you enter a noisy relationship, as manager, you tell yourself that you cannot be part of a stressful relationship. Help your Self to find the nearest exit.

Some ego-dystonic relationships may be unavoidable such as your relationship with a T1 parent, sibling, or mate. As manager, you must monitor the way you manage your Self in these relationships and protect your Self. You no longer have to get sick because you are around T1 individuals. You can manage your interactions with T1 individuals in a manner as to preserve your emotional health and wellness. This may mean limiting the length and/or frequency of your interactions with T1 individuals. You can begin by changing the mode of interaction from face-to-face to phone, post card, smoke signal, or 'drive-by' interactions where you drive by in your car and just wave as you pass. You can protect your Self as you deal with T1 individuals and it is your managerial duty to do so.

In stewardship, your job is to vigorously direct your affairs. Stewardship is characterized by action rather than contemplation or speculation. You can't simply **know** that a negative situation exists; you have to actively participate in changing the affairs of your life. Do not wait for change; change is waiting for you.

You have been appointed as steward of your life by your Creator. The Creator gave life to you and the Creator appointed you as steward over the life you were been given. The Creator expects you to take better care of your life than your record has shown. One of the greatest things you can do is realize that the Creator gave you the breath of life. You have a portion of the Creator's spirit. Now, you are steward over the life and spirit that has been placed in you. You can honor your Creator by striving to take good care of you. Give gratitude to your Creator for the blessings you have received and for things that you didn't get. Stewardship is important because it reminds you that you do exist. There was a time when you did not know that you had a Self. You are the Creator's steward of the 'Me' in you.

5. **Self Advocacy**: An advocate is one who pleads the cause of another. This tool allows you to plead the cause of your Self. You must become a

better advocate for your Self with other people. You may often be asked by others to do things or to be in multiple places at the same time. On occasion, you have to respectfully and politely say 'no'; 'I am not in a position to take on that responsibility at this time'. You have to advocate for you rather than running your Self ragged and then feeling angry and resentful.

Furthermore, plead your own cause to you. It is often you attempting to get your Self in an awkward position where you do not belong. You have to stand up and advocate against your 2nd self, and say 'no'. If you can get your 2nd self under control, you will have little difficulty advocating for your Self where others are concerned. Advocacy starts with you. Stand up and tell you when you are tired, fatigued and need to rest. Do not allow your 2nd self to falsely accuse you of being lazy and no good. Let your Self know that you will take as much time as you need to get rest and to feel restored. It is your job to consistently advocate for what represents your best interest.

6. **Effort**: This tool is vital to living in personal freedom. Imagine **knowledge** on one side of the river and **results** on the other side of the river. The **bridge** between knowledge and results is effort. You may have been standing on the knowledge side of the river for many

years, looking across at the results side of the river. While standing on the knowledge side, you spend your time contemplating and speculating about those results. You are still standing with knowledge, looking across the river at results, because you have not built the bridge called effort. Effort is the conscious exertion of power or your will. Effort is the total work done to achieve a particular result. So, if you know it but don't do it, you will not get the results you 'say' you desire. Effort puts what you 'say' to the test. If you do not put forth the effort, your journey to personal freedom will be short-lived. Ask yourself every day, 'what is the total work that I have done today to achieve my personal freedom?' You don't need to find new effort. Simply redirect 50% of the effort that you invest in T1 relationships and apply it directly to your work on personal freedom. At once, you are reducing wasted effort by 50% while increasing your exertion of power towards personal freedom by 50%. You must make a conscious exertion of power to do the work required to achieve the goal of personal freedom. Personal freedom awaits you and effort will get you there. Effort is required for personal responsibility; personal accountability; self discipline; self advocacy and stewardship. Effort is essential because without it, none of these will be accomplished.

7. **Single**: A major tool for living in personal freedom is being single. If you have experienced T1 Thinking, you believed that you were single before you got married. If you are not married, you are actually 'not married'. It doesn't mean that you are single. A T1 Thinking 30 or 40-year-old **unmarried** male living in his mother's basement is not single. A single person is one who can singularly (without the aid, or crutch, or dependence on anyone else) love him/herself and ensure his or her own spiritual and emotional well-being. This is a hallmark for living in personal freedom. In personal freedom, single persons enjoy an intimate relationship with themselves and are able to soothe themselves. Single persons have a good Emotional Quotient. They are emotionally mature. If they need something, they can go to themselves to get it. Single people can go to themselves for a hug; a kind word; support; or encouragement. If they go to themselves to get what they need and find they don't have it, they carry themselves by the hand to a place where they can get what they need. This is being single. A single person is like an HMO (Health Maintenance Organization).

An HMO is a self-contained organization and everything you need is contained within the HMO. The HMO is a single organization because it does not **depend** on outside help. Once a single person gets married, he/she remains single. You should be single for your entire life. So, when two single people get married, they are still single and legally married. They still have an ability to take full responsibility and care for each other. They do not become emotionally needy or otherwise dependent upon each other. Marriage affords an opportunity for single persons to share what they **already** have spiritually and emotionally with each other. When a person is competent in caring for themselves, caring for someone else is far less challenging.

These are the basic tools you will need to complete your journey to personal freedom. Practice your tools often. The more you practice, the more they will become an unconscious part of you. The 'Basics Homework' worksheet will help you track your progress. All of the tools are listed down the left side of the worksheet. You can write down an issue in your life, big or small **but not related to drama**, that needs your attention. This issue can be excessive weight; T1 thinking; phobia when meeting new people; excessive anxiety when applying for a new job; or anything important for you to change. Change will not happen if you are not ready for it and if you are not willing to put forth the effort that is required for change. Write the same issue in several basic tool areas or write a different issue in several tool areas for practice. Next, write down the effort you put forth to change the issue. Finally, write down your result. You will notice that adequate effort gets results. You may not arrive in personal freedom at the same time as some others, but with consistent effort and utilizing the basics, you can achieve personal freedom.

The Basics Homework

Work sheet

	ISSUE	EFFORT	RESULT
PERSONAL RESPONSIBILITY			
PERSONAL ACCOUNTABILITY			
SELF-DISCIPLINE			

	ISSUE	EFFORT	RESULT
SELF-ADVOCACY			
STEWARDSHIP			
EFFORT			
SINGLE			

11

SPIRITUALITY IN PERSONAL FREEDOM

Personal freedom and spirituality are seamlessly interconnected. You cannot have one without the other. Spirituality is the blueprint for personal freedom. Just as a healthy physical life entails growth, a healthy spiritual life also requires growth. The same way an infant or child must be fed and nourished in order to thrive and grow up healthy, you must feed and cultivate your spiritual relationship with the Creator in order to live in personal freedom. If a child does not grow and develop naturally, he or she is said to be 'delayed' or 'challenged'. So what happens to you if your spiritual growth is not nurtured? When a pool of water is stagnant, it becomes murky, infested, and sometimes begins to smell. So what happens to you if your spiritual life is stagnant? Let's start with several fundamentals of spirituality.

WHO IS THE CREATOR AND WHAT ARE THE CREATOR'S QUALITIES?

The Creator is spirit. The Creator never changes. The Creator is all powerful, all knowing, universal, just, and perfect. The Creator is love, truth, and wisdom.

DOES MY IDENTITY COME FROM THE CREATOR?

You were made in the image and likeness of the Creator. A portion of the Creator's spirit was placed into you in order to give you life. This spirit of the Creator enables you to share a relationship with your Creator. Because you are made in the Creator's image, try to live your life so that you positively reflect your Creator. You are the Creator's workmanship and you were created to produce good works.

WHAT IS SPIRITUALITY?

Spirituality is not a feeling. It is not some mystical sense of being connected to the Creator. Spirituality is a discipline. Spirituality is a **conscious practice** of living according to the highest ethical ideals in your everyday life and it is that continued practice that brings you into a **conscious contact** with your Creator. This means that you have to show love, patience, kindness, forgiveness, honesty, trustworthiness, etc. Do unto others, as you would have them do unto you.

Love your brother and sister as you love yourself. Spirituality is preceded by spiritual growth.

Spiritual growth is a choice. It does not happen by default. You can't sleep with an 'Inspirational Text' under your pillow and expect a transfer of information. You must invest time in your personal relationships in order for them to be healthy. Likewise, you also need to spend time with the Creator to have a close and healthy relationship. If you have a friend that you never call; you never thank him or her for favors; you never give him or her credit for things that they make possible in your life; how close do you feel your relationship will be with that person? No matter how busy you are, you have to make time to contact that friend and cultivate or look after that relationship in order for it to be healthy and intimate. Intimate means someone that you can depend on to be there for you when everyone else leaves; Someone who supports you when others brand you a failure; Someone who you can tell your most personal thoughts and issues and will not be judgmental or repeat what you say; Someone who loves you in spite of your faults and only wants to see you succeed; and someone who knows the REAL you and still accepts that you are capable of greatness.

You may be saying to yourself, 'Self, I don't have a friend like that'. Well, you can have that kind of a friend. It is a choice and this is how can you make that choice.

Spiritual growth requires **concentrated** effort. Like physical health, spiritual growth requires regular exercise. It is not easy. You must work at it; today; tomorrow; and always. The first pre-requisite for spiritual growth is a true and personal relationship with the Creator. Remember, **Spiritual Growth is a Choice**. Make a decision and formulate a plan to help you achieve your goal. It is a choice. You are capable of developing an effective and fulfilling spiritual life. Here are six practical keys that will help you to develop spiritual growth:

1. **Control your thoughts**. You must learn to master your thoughts or train of thought. If you cannot control your thoughts, your thoughts will completely govern your behavior. At a given time each day, it is important that you have a quiet period where you become so absorbed in your healthy thoughts and reaffirming ideas, that no other thoughts can enter into your mind and disturb your spirit. Learn how to listen to the 'still small voice' within you. Feed your spirit with positive images and read passages that offer an infusion of healthy emotional nutrients. The Creator says that you are beautifully and wonderfully made. If your Creator says positive things about you, why would you allow what people say to have more influence? Develop your relationship so that you can hear what your Creator says about you and it will overshadow the negativity coming from anyone else, including you. Work at it---today---tomorrow---always.

2. **Control your actions.** Controlling your actions requires **much effort**! This is not about controlling your actions in an external environment like your workplace, civic group, among people you respect, etc. It is

important for you to have internal control of your actions, no matter how important or how insignificant the matter may be. You exercise internal control when you don't punch, slap, spit on, kick, or curse at your spiritual leader for saying or doing something you don't agree with. Spiritual growth requires you to exercise this kind of internal control with everyone. Do you really believe in a Creator that is far greater than yourself? Do you believe that the Creator can enable you to have self control? The way to really show that you believe in your Creator is to allow yourself to be led. Allow the Creator to do what you need and believe the Creator can do it for you. Stop putting your hands in it and thinking that you can do it on your own. Do the decisions you've made and the solutions that you've come up with at this point in your life indicate that you are equipped to go it alone?

3. **Equanimity.** Learn to stay on an even keel. You tend to fluctuate back and forth between joy and sorrow, and allow yourself to be rocked by the waves of life. The goal here is to become steadfast and even-tempered. Don't get too high with your successes or too low with your failures. Make sure your reaction fits the situation. If you punch a hole in the wall because Burger King didn't put pickles on your hamburger, something's wrong with that. If you start turning somersaults

because you found a dollar on the ground, something's wrong with that. If you become depressed and stay in a darkened room under the covers because someone didn't speak to you, something's wrong with that. If you think you are in love after knowing someone for two weeks...If you hate your boss because she wants you to do your job... You get the picture.

4. **Have Compassion.** Try to find the good in any situation. Try to understand your shortcomings. Look for opportunities to reaffirm you. 'Every cloud has a silver lining.' Look at the silver lining instead of looking at the cloud. The goal of an effective spiritual life is not to be perfect, but to strive for perfection. When you mess up, know that at least you were trying to do something positive. If you know that you didn't try your hardest, admit it. Tell yourself that you can and you will do better. Encourage yourself. Don't beat your Self up. There are enough people already lining up to do that. (Remember the movie **Airplane**...)

5. **Complete Openness.** Don't judge new things according to old things that you already know. Don't confront new information immediately with your own opinion. Always remain open to learning something new. Develop the ability to listen. Effective communication is <u>more</u>

dependent on your ability to listen and hear what someone else is saying, instead of being able to articulate what you think or feel. Let's be clear. Communicating your feelings is of utmost importance in avoiding misunderstandings; but being able to hear what someone else is saying is extremely important. This only refers to hearing someone who is speaking positive things into your spirit that can help you become a better you. Listen to what is presented as constructive criticism. Once you hear what they are saying then you can decide if it's nonsense. Take the time to listen with an open mind and let your decision be based on all the information.

6. **Inner Harmony.** This comes from developing the first five keys. As you perfect these other qualities, you begin to achieve inner harmony. You develop spiritual, mental, emotional, and physical balance. You are at peace within. The peace of your Creator will guard your heart and mind.

There are blessings that come with spiritual growth and having an intimate relationship with your Creator: love, peace of mind (in the midst of turmoil), rejoicing in hope (knowing that nothing is too hard for your Creator), virtue (trustworthiness and honesty), knowledge (understanding of the order of things), self-control (self discipline or strength of will), patience, kindness, and faithfulness. These blessings lead to a more fulfilled and abundant life.

The Creator desires to complete the work that was started when you were created. The Creator strengthens you in your efforts to grow and equips you with unimaginable power! There is no excuse not to grow---beyond the limits that you think will hinder you.

Spiritual growth is a life-long process. Surrounding yourself with others who are also seeking to increase their spiritual development will greatly increase your chance of success. If you find yourself becoming more loving, more joyful, kinder, and having more self-control, you can rest assured that spiritual growth is genuinely occurring in your life. Five indicators of spiritual development are gratitude, compassion, forgiveness, detachment, and truth.

An intimate spiritual relationship with the Creator becomes a rock that you can hang on to when you feel the world is spinning out of control. It gives you the courage to push on when you don't want to and it shows you the way when it seems there is no way. With spirituality, you rest easy knowing that whatever ails you, enrages you, troubles you, or gets on your nerves, you can overcome it. Spirituality will enable you to cheer up when you feel down. It lightens you up, even when you are hurt. This is not to say that an intimate relationship with the Creator will prevent you from being presented with drama, but it will help you minimize the effects of the drama in your life. It will help you control your participation in the drama. It will help you lessen the impact of others' negativity. It will help you remain optimistic in the face of an extremely stressful or bleak situation. It will also help you love yourself so that you can love others as well. Spiritual growth is not an option, it is a necessity! It is a necessity to live in personal freedom.

12

PERSONAL FREEDOM

Personal freedom belongs to you. You were born with personal freedom. You were living in personal freedom prior to the first change in your thinking at age 5. At age 5, you began to misplace your personal freedom, but you never lost possession of it. You searched the world trying to recover personal freedom which is an inherent part of your Self. Your journey has taken you through turmoil and confusion. Your Self has been exposed to dirt, mud, muck, and mire, but it is still unchanged and still in mint condition. If you place gold in dirt, mud, muck, and mire and you take it out, it's still gold. It's just as valuable as it was before it was misplaced. The same can be said for your Self. It has been rough, but the search is over now. It is true that you never lost possession of your Self. You just didn't have anyone to tell you. The people that were supposed to show you how to hold on to and treasure your Self were lost themselves. Rather than blame and beat your Self up, celebrate your resilience for being willing to spare no limit, good or bad, to rediscover your Self.

Learning to live in personal freedom again will not be easy. Can you think of anything in life worth having that is easy? You are worth it. Reclaiming your personal freedom will be a challenge, but take advantage of the opportunity.

Personal freedom will feel like a new way of life. You will need time to adjust to living in freedom. For instance, personal freedom offers **choice**. You have the ability to choose between right and wrong, good and bad. You don't have real choice when there is only good or only bad. You would be like a human robot doing all good or all bad. In personal freedom, you are free to select among varied choices. In personal freedom, more often than not, you will choose what represents your best interest and the best interest of others.

Your journey from T1 relationships to personal freedom is a **process**, not an event. Some people do not like process; don't understand the importance of process; or would love to be able to skip the process and go straight to the outcome. Your willingness to embrace process is a strong predictor of your achieving personal freedom. This process involves taking your Self through an established set of steps to convert your T1 Thinking to healthy thinking. The **process** is as important as the outcome produced by the process. You cannot fully appreciate the results of personal freedom without completing the process. Personal freedom is your destination and process is the vehicle that will get you there. Therefore, it is important that you not become ambivalent, lackadaisical, forgetful, or negligent of your vehicle. You cannot stop in the middle of the process. There is a quotation on an outside wall of Union Station in Washington, DC that says: "On the plains of hesitation, bleach the bones of countless millions who, at the dawn of victory, paused to rest, and while resting, died". You must stay on course and finish your process. If you give half-hearted effort, your results will be half-hearted. If you grow weary and say that the process is too hard, then you will be left behind. The process of personal freedom includes:

- Studying your definitions in the glossary of this book;
- Utilizing the 'empty chair technique' or a mirror to have conversations with you;
- Avoiding complacency;
- Practicing the 'is my relationship with Me sinking' exercise;
- Practicing spiritual growth;
- Practicing the Basics using the homework sheet;
- Practicing my Will and my Importance exercises;
- Practicing 'the things that you need to do for you';
- Practicing KFOM using the daily checklist;
- Practicing interactions with healthy individuals; and
- Participating in self-help groups, consultation with a behavioral health professional and/or a spiritual leader.

You are encouraged to devote a minimum of 10 hours per week to your process. There are several things you can learn from this 10 hour/week process. You can learn whether or not you can depend on yourself. You can learn whether or not you are committed to achieving personal freedom. You can also learn what you must **know** and **believe,** and **will** for yourself to live in personal freedom.

If you discipline yourself to complete the process, you will develop many of the skills required to live in personal freedom. Your right to live in personal freedom comes with responsibilities.

Personal freedom means that you are free to **be** and to love your Self, unconditionally. No one is perfect and we all have some experiences we would like to undo. However, personal freedom allows you to love your Self despite any mistakes that you made in the past; despite any mistakes you make today; and despite any mistakes you might make tomorrow. Learning how to love your Self includes the ability to lovingly detach from people who are important, but not healthy for you. You cannot remain connected to some of your T1 relationships and live in personal freedom. You must take your Self out of harm's way, as far away as possible from these negative relationships. You will be asked to go places and do things by people important to you. Once you begin to live in personal freedom, you will notice that you spend less time in old familiar places and engaging in old behaviors. Personal freedom is also about learning how to safely love those who do not know how to love themselves. You will lose some T1 people who have subtracted from you and divided you. You will engage new healthy people who add to you and enhance you. While every human being has a birth right to live in personal freedom, only those who **want**

to live in personal freedom and put forth the required effort will do so. Some T1 individuals will forfeit their birth right. Remember, personal freedom is not free. It comes with responsibility.

Personal freedom means that you trust your Self. You can trust you to no longer place your Self in precarious situations that do not represent your best interest. Now ask yourself up front, 'is that person; that place; or that thing good for me?' If the answer is 'no', you trust your Self enough not to get involved. If you can trust your Self, you can trust others who are **trustworthy**. You can no longer trust 'Shaky' (the known thief, robber, and crook) to safeguard your money for you; and then get angry at him when he does what 'Shaky' does; that is, disappear with your money. Those without a demonstrated history of trustworthiness cannot receive your trust. Your trust in others can no longer be misplaced. Trust is a precious commodity possessed by a few. Learn to trust your Self; then, the 'few' will become known to you.

Personal freedom allows you to enjoy an intimate relationship with your Self. An intimate relationship with your Self says that you are present and available to you. You are **one** with your Self. You are no longer split between 'Me' and 2nd self. If you need encouragement, a pat on the back, or a hug, you are the first person to show up to meet your needs. You don't have to wait for someone else to show up or wait until you meet a person who may or may not be willing or able to meet your needs. You can also share your intimate relationship with others who have an intimate relationship with themselves.

Personal freedom offers you autonomy of thought and peace of mind. You deserve to have peace of mind. You have walked around for years with scenes of war, nightmares and horror stories in your mind. Peace of mind is freedom from disturbing and oppressive thoughts. These distressing experiences cannot exist in your mind while you live in personal freedom. Your thoughts are now consumed with optimism, positivity, and **hope.** In personal freedom, you no longer allow negative people to consume your thoughts. You can focus your thoughts on who and what is in your best interest.

Personal freedom requires you to be **willing** to live in personal freedom without your T1 mate. Are you willing to live in personal freedom without your T1 mate? You cannot base your freedom upon the decisions of your T1mate. You must choose for yourself and allow your mate the right to decide. You can make your own choice and you must be clear about the choice you make. Just remember, you cannot live in personal freedom with anyone who decides to remain in emotional bondage.

Personal freedom allows you freedom to dream. This dream is about seeing your Self fulfilling your raison d'être. You have often wondered 'why am I here?' Your freedom to dream **reveals** your reason for being. You also have vision which is the process that will take you to your dreams. Your dreams in personal freedom show you where you are going and your vision in personal freedom shows you how you will get there.

Personal freedom allows you to pass what has been freely given to you on to others, particularly children. Children need healthy adults who can mirror who they are. Children look to healthy adults to help define them Selves. Children develop a healthy Self through interacting with healthy adults in their lives. One of the greatest gifts you can share with children is your relationship with your Self. Let a child see the 'Me' in you. Help a child know and connect with his/her own 'me'. If the child is an infant or toddler, they're already living in personal freedom and only need consistent, healthy reactions from you. If the child is older and has already developed T1 Thinking, help the young person begin to accurately interpret his/her T1 environment. You can serve as a consistent source of truthful information for a child, whether it is your own, a niece or nephew, or a child from the neighborhood. You can help a child understand the difference between their facts and their truth. This will help a young person to avoid depression, eating disorders, drug abuse and other behavioral problems.

Sharing your Self with a child is important because whatever is happening to parents and adult caretakers is also happening to their children. Children will spend their time learning and exploring their 'me' or raiding the family medicine cabinet for prescription drugs. Children do drugs not to feel at all or to feel better. The best antidote to efforts to escape 'reality' is to consistently help children to know who they are. If you don't help them, drug dealers, pimps, and charismatic anti-social individuals will gladly take time to continue to misinform and mislead children. Consider it your duty and responsibility to help save a child from T1 Thinking. Help them know their resilience, strength, innocence, intrinsic value, and how to love themselves. Let them know they do not have to duplicate the mistakes of their T1parents and caretakers. T1parents want their children to be happy and successful, but they simply don't know how to help their children realize their dreams. Now, you can help save a child. When you save one child, you also save the next generation of children.

Personal freedom means spiritual freedom. You are free to discover, every day, more about the Creator's plan for your life. You should distance yourself from your plan and begin to follow the Creator's plan for your life. You have learned that your plan for your life has not and will not work. A perfect plan for your life has already been created and you cannot improve it, although you have tried very hard to do so. Personal freedom is to experience the full promises and rewards the Creator has already prepared for you. It is important that you be properly positioned to receive these blessings. Once you reconnect to the Creator's plan for your life, you can be comforted in knowing that no obstacle will prevent you from receiving what the Creator has already planned for you. The economy, high unemployment rates, high interest rates, or national shortages become less terrifying because you know that you are following the Creator's plan for your life. When you step outside your Creator's plan, you do have cause for concern. You are on your own with no guarantee of getting back to your Creator's plan for your life.

As long as you live, you will have personal freedom. In order to resume your life in personal freedom, you have to **know it**; **believe it**; and have the **will to live** in personal freedom. It's about choice. You can actually choose to live in personal freedom or live as a prisoner of your own thinking. No one can or should make this choice for you. It is completely up to you. Exercise your freedom of choice to rededicate yourself and reconnect to a healthy relationship with your Self; your Creator; and to share your relationships with others. Enjoy your freedom.

Personal Freedom Progress Report Worksheet

Please rate yourself in the following key areas of personal freedom (1 is low and 10 is high):

1.	FREEDOM OF EMOTION	1 2 3 4 5 6 7 8 9 10
2.	FREEDOM TO LOVE T1 OTHERS AT A DISTANCE	1 2 3 4 5 6 7 8 9 10
3.	I TRUST MYSELF	1 2 3 4 5 6 7 8 9 10
4.	I HAVE AN INTIMATE RELATIONSHIP WITH MYSELF	1 2 3 4 5 6 7 8 9 10
5.	I HAVE SPIRITUAL FREEDOM	1 2 3 4 5 6 7 8 9 10
6.	I HAVE PEACE OF MIND	1 2 3 4 5 6 7 8 9 10
7.	I AM OPTIMISTIC ABOUT MY FUTURE	1 2 3 4 5 6 7 8 9 10
8.	WHAT I KNOW AND WHO I AM ARE ONE	1 2 3 4 5 6 7 8 9 10
9.	I AM WILLING TO RECOVER WITHOUT MY MATE	1 2 3 4 5 6 7 8 9 10
10.	I AM ACCOUNTABLE FOR MY OWN RECOVERY	1 2 3 4 5 6 7 8 9 10

Complete the questionnaire in 90 day intervals. The goal is to eventually achieve a minimum rating of 7 in all areas.

Utilize this worksheet to measure your progress at 90 day intervals. It is important to discuss your results with a healthy thinking person, spiritual leader, and/or a behavioral health professional. You may also participate in NDR groups via webinars, teleconferences and groups held in your local area. You will need time before you are able to evaluate your own self-assessment. Moreover, your progress in personal freedom will become evident to you when it is brought to your attention by others who live in personal freedom. This will be the final piece of evidence to show that you have worked to repair the damage to your Self and that you are back in good rapport with your 'Me'. For as long as you shall live, purpose never to lose or misplace your 'Me' ever again.

CLOSING PRAYER

God, I pray that You would help me to let go of my T1 Thinking, so that I can live according to Your will.

Help me to clearly see my T1 Thinking patterns.

Help me to Learn; to **Trust**; and to **Believe** in **Your Truth** and have the **Will** to **consistently** practice **Your Truth** for **my life**.

As a result, I believe that I will discover unconditional love for You, myself and others; and I will experience joy, emotional sobriety, and peace of mind.

I will also be able to say, 'I Am who God says I Am' and begin to walk in the path that God has already prepared for 'Me'.

Today, I Proclaim, I am Free and I am able to live in Personal Freedom!

GLOSSARY OF TERMS

T1 Thinking – The first significant change in one's thinking. Powerfully negative thoughts developed in early childhood and based upon misinformation usually received from primary care-takers. These negative thoughts set the stage for addictive behaviors and/or addictive relationships. Individuals who never used alcohol or drugs, but have maintained important relationships with substance abusers, usually have T1 Thinking and can be more difficult to treat than substance abusers. These persons have been referred to as people pleasers, enablers, and co-dependents.

T2 Thinking- Second significant change in one's thinking. Person also pursues the abuse of drugs, alcohol, food, and other addictive behaviors (in part) to escape and to manage the powerfully negative emotions related to their T1 thinking. T2 individuals attempt to medicate (soothe) their feelings with alcohol, drugs, food, sex or gambling.

T 1 Relationship- An unhealthy collision between individuals who are: T1 and T1; T1 and T2; or T2 and T2. Addictive relationships are usually unrewarding, unsuccessful, and characterized by Drama!!! These individuals can remain at war with each other in these unhealthy relationships for 20 years or more despite little evidence that their relationship will ever yield peace and happiness for themselves or their children.

Fantasy- The process of creating unrealistic or improbable mental images as an attempt to fulfill one's psychological needs. Fantasy can **never** be reality. T 1 relationships are usually based on fantasy.

T1 Network- The broader group of significant others and associates with whom we maintain unhealthy relationships and negative thinking. These may include family members or anyone who is T1 or T2.

Drama - Intense verbal and sometimes physical interaction between T1 and/or T2 individuals that results from unmet fantasies. These individuals blame each other for not doing for them that which **could not be done**.

Addict - An Addict is a person who devotes him or herself to 'someThing' or to 'someOne' **habitually** or **obsessively**. Many Addicts are T1 individuals who no longer or never abused substances but remain addicted to PEOPLE who are important to them.

Sober - The absence of an outside substance used to alter one's thinking and emotions. Many sober individuals unknowingly remain T1 for many years after ceasing alcohol or drug abuse.

Stuck On Sober - Individuals who have ceased alcohol or drug abuse for many years but continue to unknowingly experience T1 Thinking and involvement in other addictions that include Food, Sex, Gambling or **PEOPLE**.

Sobriety - Quality thinking wherein at least 7 out of 10 thoughts are positive, constructive, and productive for the individual and people around him/her. Sobriety allows individuals to be at peace with themselves and others. All people can and deserve the opportunity to Live in Sobriety.

Choice - The ability to conceive and select among a variety of healthy or unhealthy options. People who think healthy usually make healthy choices. However, people who think negatively usually select from a wide selection of unhealthy predetermined decisions.

Yuv (pronounced luv) - A psychological defense used to justify behavior that would otherwise clearly be Insane!!!

Love - The ability to first give unconditional trust, intimacy, affection, and support to Oneself, then relate to others as you relate to yourself.

Freedom - An ability to live and grow in harmony with oneself, others, and the Creator.

Marriage - A close and intimate union. T1 individuals usually have little Evidence to validate or support their claim of marriage. The evidence routinely indicates that the 'marriage' primarily serves a legal purpose.

Transference - The unconscious redirection of feelings from an important childhood relationship to a present relationship. T1 individuals usually continue to live in the **past** via their **present** relationships with their T1mates and T1significant others.

Projective Identification – The process of placing what we dislike in ourselves into someone else and then holding that person responsible for how we feel. Sometimes we can project positive feelings into another person in an attempt to control them and to get what we need from them.

T1 Distortion - Unrealistic perceptions based upon false beliefs regarding myself and persons important to me, that I continue to believe despite contradicting Evidence and

Facts. T1 individuals usually have troubled relationships with significant others i.e., mates, family members, etc.

Mate - One of a matched pair. T1 individuals often mistakenly refer to their mates as husbands, wives, and other terms of endearment.

Ego-Centric - One who limits his or her outlook or concerns to his or her Own needs. T1 individuals have an understanding of what they need emotionally but cannot understand that their Mates are not capable of meeting their emotional needs.

Denial - A psychological defense mechanism in which confrontation with a personal problem or reality is AVOIDED by REFUSING to accept the existence, truth or validity of the problem or reality. (from the little BIG book dictionary) Denial is a constant process.

Projection - We take something that we like, dislike or need in ourselves and falsely believe that our likes, dislikes or needs actually come from another person.

Fear- An unpleasant and often strong emotion caused by the anticipation or awareness of real danger. People cannot experience fear when the danger is not real.

Phobia- An exaggerated and illogical fear of a particular situation. Phobia feels the same as fear except that fear is based in reality whereas phobia is based in one's perception.

Important - Indicative of significant worth; valuable in relationship.

Will- The power or control over one's own action or emotion.

T1 Knowledge- A defense mechanism that protects one from reality, fear, insecurity and change. Intellectualization is the power of **Knowing,** which is different from the power of **Believing** and the power to **Will**. So, just because we **know it** does not mean we have the **belief** and **will** to **do it.**

Belief- The state or habit of mind in which trust (or confidence) is placed in some person or some being or phenomenon, especially when based on examination of **EVIDENCE.**

Doubt – Uncertainty of Belief or an opinion that interferes with decision-making. It is a deliberate suspension of judgment and gives rise to uncertainty, hesitation, suspense (anxiety) lack of confidence, distrust and an inclination **NOT** to believe or to accept.

Alter-Ego - A 2nd Self; A trusted 'friend'.

Self-Control- Restraint exercised over one's own impulses, thoughts and emotions.

Personal Responsibility- It is my job alone to take care of me and to make sure that I'm ok spiritually, mentally and emotionally.

Personal Accountability- I must be able to provide a justifiable explanation (not another excuse) for my behavior and actions.

Stewardship- The individual's responsibility to manage and actively direct his/her own affairs of life with Skill and Care.

Negative Attachments- a seemingly natural attraction to negative people, places and things that show little evidence of being in your best interest.

Self Advocacy- One who pleads the cause for himself and for herself.

Effort- The total work done to achieve a particular end.

Distortion- To twist out of the TRUE meaning.

Complacency- Satisfaction that is accompanied by unawareness (denial) of the Actual dangers or deficiencies.

Krazy- Full of cracks or flaws; unsound; impractical; and **Out of the Ordinary**

ACCLAIM FOR DR. COLLINS'

"A Journey from T1 Relationships to Personal Freedom"

Awesome! This book helped me to change my life! It has taught me how to recognize and respond to T1 relationships and T1 thinkers at home, work, and family gatherings. This book is a must read for teenagers, young adults and older adults!

— **LISA CARTWRIGHT, SYSTEMS SECURITY ENGINEER**

A very down to earth roadmap for redirection of one's life journey heretofore littered with hazardous obstacles. This literary work of art encourages critical introspection of lifelong harmful habits/relationships. It places, into proper perspective, reasons for perceived failures throughout one's life. Most humbling is his acknowledgement of the Creator to whom all reverence should be directed. I congratulate Dr. Collins for this well composed project.

— **LEE A. HUTTON, JR., M.D.**

This book has given me insight and clarity about where I've been, how I got there, and how to move on towards personal freedom, one day at a time. I now know how to love God, myself, and my neighbor.

I encourage anyone who is tired of being unhappy and feeling stuck to read this book. I've read many self help books; however, this book is superior to all. We can let go of the pain, and begin living an abundant life filled with purpose, tranquility, and love.

— GWEN T.

Thank you for writing this book, Dr. Collins. The information in this book has been a blue print that enabled me to walk away from a lifetime of bondage to patterns of thinking and behavior that caused me nothing but pain in several areas of my life. I have been able to reclaim my personal freedom by recognizing that when I do the "Basics", the miracles of recovery show up in my life. I have lost 242 pounds of excess weight. I have put down credit cards and stopped outspending my income. My adult children are free to make decisions in their lives without any interference or 'guidance' from me.

Today, I am not always right. I can be corrected. I am not close to perfect. I take responsibility for living by the highest spiritual principles I can when no one is watching but me, and accept with good grace, when I fall short. In other words, today, I mostly live in peace.

May God continue to bless you.

— MARIETTA M.

Captivating! Once you start reading, you can't put it down. This book provided answers regarding behaviors I could not understand. It inspired me to grow spiritually! This book is a must read for anyone who is in search of meaning and purpose of life. Dr. Collins helps you rediscover your True Self and teaches you how to live in harmony with your Self and the rest of the world!

— **OKSANA KAZHAROVA, MSW, LCSW, LCADC**

In the past, I have struggled to be free spiritually, mentally, and emotionally, but I always felt stuck. I just couldn't figure out life's riddles. After reading and practicing the information in this book, I have awakened to the truth about my thinking. My thinking was plagued by denial of the real dangers and deficiencies which always showed up in my behavior.

I must say that my thinking was hazy and my mind's eye needed new lenses. Thanks to this book, I can see so much more clearly! I am presently growing in harmony with myself, others, and my Creator. Thank you Dr. Collins. This book is truly a God send! Thank you for your dedication, strait talk, and most of all, for your passion to help ordinary people like me.

— **JAMES E. L., NDR GRADUATE**

This book transforms the spiritual principles of recovery into concrete principles. It shows how to free oneself to be the human being our Creator intended us to be. I thank Dr. Collins because his book helped me to realign my will with the WILL of the Creator who has made mankind in the best of molds (95:4).

— **ADIB R. ABDULLAH, MA**

AUTHOR INFORMATION

-Dr. Winston Collins, University of Pennsylvania, LCSW, QCSW, DCSW.
-Director of Addictive Behavior Division at a leading Behavioral Health Center in Philadelphia, Pa.
-Precision Consultants of Philadelphia, Private Practice.
-Associate Professorships at Bryn Marw University and Community College of Philadelphia (1981 to 1987)
Memberships and Affiliations:
NASW; Philadelphia Bar Association; Expert Witness, Federal Defenders of Eastern Pennsylvania; Senior Evaluator, Pa Board of Law Examiners; Senior Evaluator, ACCESS EAP; Senior Evaluator, Lawyers Concerned for Lawyers; Board of Directors, Homemaker Services of Philadelphia; and founder, Next Dimension Recovery (NDR).
He is also an accomplished bass player and member of the Omega Psi Phi Fraternity, Inc.
Book Publications:
"A Journey from T1 Relationships to Personal Freedom" by CreateSpace Independent Publishing Platform, (2014). Next Dimension Recovery Press.

23792631R00086

Made in the USA
Middletown, DE
03 September 2015